ISE Appraisal &

Database Management Systems Volume

March 1990

LONDON: HMSO

ISE Appraisal and Evaluation
Application Generators Volume

© **Crown Copyright 1990**

First published 1990

ISBN 0 11 330533 8

For further information regarding this document please contact :-

Information Systems Engineering Division
CCTA, Norwich
0603 694762

Foreword

This document is the Database Management Systems volume of the CCTA Information Systems Engineering Appraisal and Evaluation Library. This Library is intended to be used to aid appraisal and evaluation of data management products and consists of an Overview and Procedures Volume, together with supporting technology specific volumes.

The Overview and Procedures Volume describes the series and provides a procedure for using the criteria contained in the technology specific volumes in a number of contexts. These include making a strategic selection, evaluation during a feasibility study, and evaluation during the procurement stage of a project. The evaluation procedure is placed into the context of other CCTA procedures, such as those for procurement and evaluation, and methods such as SSADM. It has been written in support of the CCTA Information Systems Guides.

Each technology specific volume provides a hierarchy of criteria that may be used as the basis for the evaluation of products in that technology class. The initial volumes will be for Application Generators, Knowledge Based Systems, and Application Software Packages; as well as this volume for Database Management Systems.

This Appraisal and Evaluation Library has been produced to assist organisations to identify the product, or set of products, which best meets their requirements. The procedure and the criteria have developed as technology has changed, and as a result of experience gained from their use. CCTA welcomes comment on, and contributions to, this Library to ensure that it continues to provide maximum benefit.

ISE Appraisal and Evaluation
Database Management Systems Volume

Contents

Introduction   page

i	**General**	7
ii	**Scope**	11
iii	**Criteria**	19

Chapter

1	**Data structure and handling**	23
	1.1 Data definition (schema)	23
	1.2 Data definition (schema) manipulation	28
	1.3 Data manipulation	29
2	**Portability**	35
	2.1 DBMS portability	35
	2.2 Schema portability	35
	2.3 Data portability	35
	2.4 Skill mobility	36
3	**Serviceability**	37
	3.1 Multi user capabilities	37
	3.2 Recovery	38
	3.3 Resilience	43
	3.4 Integrity	44
4	**Performance**	51
	4.1 Characteristics for management information systems	51
	4.2 Characteristics for on-line TP systems	52
	4.3 Characteristics for batch systems	53
	4.4 Characteristics for mixed systems	53
	4.5 Tuning facilities	53
	4.6 Recovery performance	59
5	**Control and security**	61
	5.1 Ownership	61
	5.2 Operational controls	61
	5.3 Control over access to data	61
	5.4 Development control	63
	5.5 Security	64

6		**Data distribution**	65
	6.1	Distributed processing	65
	6.2	Distributed database	65
7		**Structured Systems Analysis and Design Methodology**	73
	7.1	Compatibility	73
	7.2	Tool support of SSADM	75
8		**Product credibility**	77
	8.1	Quality of product	77
	8.2	Product development status	77
	8.3	Supplier assessment	78
	8.4	Product background	79
	8.5	Documentation	83
	8.6	Training	84
	8.7	Support	84
	8.8	Enhancements	87
9		**Utilisation of recent technical developments**	89
	9.1	Hardware and system integrated DBMSs	89
	9.2	Multi processor hardware	89
	9.3	Client/server	90
10		**System development and productivity tools**	91
	10.1	Application generator capabilities	91
	10.2	Integration with development tools	91
	10.3	3GL development support	94
	10.4	Development cycle support	95
	10.5	End user tools	96
	10.6	Data conversion, loading and migration tools	96
11		**Project specific requirements**	99
12		**Costs**	101
	12.1	Software	101
	12.2	Hardware	102
	12.3	System development, operation and maintenance	102
	12.4	People	103
Annex		**Criteria hierarchy**	105

i General

i.1 Background

This document is the technology specific volume on Database Management Systems from the CCTA Appraisal and Evaluation Library of volumes on the subject of application development product appraisal and evaluation.

The objective of this Library is to define a framework for

> 'impartial and effective evaluation to find the product, or products, which best meet the needs and constraints of the organisation.'

The CCTA Information Systems Engineering Division first produced a guide to the Appraisal and Evaluation of Application Generator and Database Management System (DBMS) products in 1986. This document was updated in 1988, in the process being divided into two volumes, one for Application Generators and one for DBMS.

Several other subject areas have been identified where evaluation criteria may usefully be provided. To avoid duplication of content the common, procedural element, has been separate out into a separate Overview and Procedures volume as part of the Library.

This volume provides technology specific evaluation criteria appropriate to DBMS products. It should be used in conjunction with the Overview and Procedures volume.

i.2 The importance of Database Management Systems

This volume is intended to help in the appraisal and evaluation of DBMS software. The pace of software development in the late 1980's has helped to create a systems environment for the success of DBMS products. Because this development has taken place in a highly competitive software marketplace, with open procurement policies, means that implementors, as customers, have opportunities for wide choice.

Data management products are becoming increasingly important; in particular because of their ability to

ISE Appraisal and Evaluation
Database Management Systems Volume

produce high quality, easily maintainable computer systems, faster, and with reduced reliance upon highly skilled technical staff. It does not follow however that the need for thorough systems analysis and design can be dispensed with. Application Generators (AG) are used to develop the applications, and Database Management System (DBMS) are used to implement and maintain the data content.

AG and DBMS products can be obtained from a number of suppliers, and products from different suppliers can be used together. Therefore separate Application Generator and Database Management Systems volumes have been produced to allow the separate, independent, evaluation of both types of products. The separate assessment of the DBMS and AG components of the software environment reflect the movement of many vendors towards providing 'open systems', in which different components of the environment can be produced by different software vendors. Other software components such as end user Query Facilities and Report Writers will probably also exist within the environment but are likely to be of lesser importance.

i.3   Audience

The main audience for this document is Information Technology (IT) staff wishing to carry out appraisals or evaluations for soundly based procurement.

This volume will also be of interest to senior IT management considering the introduction of Database Management products and wishing to ensure that such introduction is carried out professionally, resulting in the selection of the most appropriate product.

It is assumed that the reader has at least a basic understanding of data processing, the role of recommended standard methods such as PRINCE and SSADM and of hardware architecture. Knowledge of data management is not assumed, with introduction ii providing some background information and explanation of the terminology used in this volume.

Because of these assumptions experienced data management practitioners may find the volume too descriptive in some parts, but technically simplified in others. It should be remembered, however, that the document will be used as a primer by those unfamiliar with the topic, and also serving as a useful reference document for experienced people.

i.4 **Expected uses**

It is expected that the volumes in this Library will be used in several ways. The uses identified in the Overview and Procedures Volume are:

- strategic, business-based, evaluation of products to select a 'standard' product for subsequent organisation wide use

- less detailed evaluation of products as an element of a feasibility study

- full evaluation of products during procurement for a project

- independent appraisal of a product.

i.5 **Structure of this volume**

This document is in three parts - introductions, the evaluation criteria, and an annex.

This is the first introduction. Introduction ii describes the scope of the subject area and explains the terminology. Introduction iii describes the notation used for the criteria, and summarises the main headings.

The bulk of the document contains the high level criteria and the checklists of detailed technical questions used within the evaluation model to assess and rank DBMS products. The questions can be used as an aide-memoire when gathering information about products.

The annex contains a hierarchy chart of the subject matter in this volume. This chart may be used as a default or as the basis for a hierarchy chart which best meets the needs of the project or organisation.

i.6 **Outline of the procedure**

The evaluation process comprises 7 stages are described in the Overview and Procedures Volume.

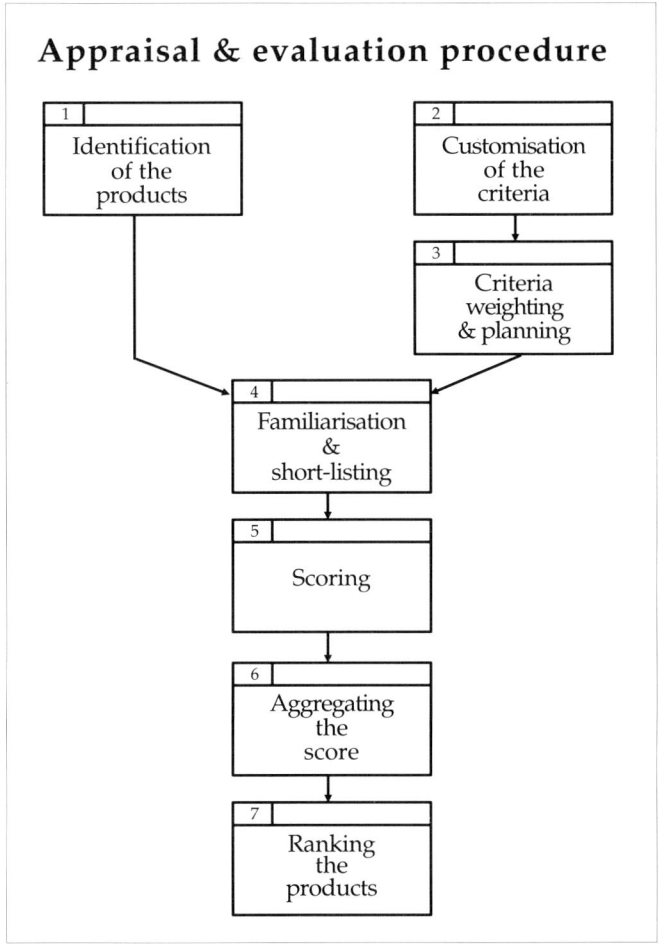

i.7 **History**

This DBMS volume supersedes ISE Report No. 33 - 'Database Management Systems - Appraisal and Evaluation', and the earlier report - 'Application Generator - Assessment Evaluation and Selection', these were published in 1988 and 1986 respectively. The content of this volume has been revised in the light of experience gained through being used in several major procurements and for technical appraisals of data management products. To make the volume easier to use detailed technical questions have been interspersed with the criteria.

ii Scope

ii.1 Scope of the volume

The evaluation criteria in this volume relate to Database Management System (DBMS) software products appropriate for the construction of multi user databases. The method is particularly suited to, and has been used on both strategic and tactical procurements (See the Overview and Procedures volume for further details)..

The term 'Database Management System' refers to data management products capable of supporting shared usage of data by a number of concurrent users. Smaller applications, especially those which do not require real time updating of data, may find one of the simpler file management systems (also often described as a database system) more cost effective.

ii.2 AG and DBMS definition

The 'Data Management' arena can be very confusing for a beginner because of the multiplicity and contradictory nature of the terminology used by the product vendors and in the press. It is impossible to give a precise definition of many terms such as '4GL' and '4GE'. New terms are invented frequently and new products are developed which transcend existing demarcations. We endeavour to set out here, in a simple fashion, definitions of terms used in this document.

Below is set out in a simple fashion, the definitions used in this volume. The fundamental distinction we can make is between the front-end application oriented elements and the back-end data management elements, with some form of data control or 'query' language controlling the communication between them. There is no necessity for the front and back-ends to come from the same vendor, indeed many vendors do not supply both.

Front-end

Typically the front-end will include several different elements used initially for developing applications and subsequently by the application when it is running. These elements may be grouped together and sold as a package, often collectively being called the 'Application Generator' (AG), or may be sold individually or in small groups. The complete front-end may alternatively be known as a Fourth Generation Environment (4GE), or as a Fourth Generation System (4GS). Note that this library classes the fourth generation language as a component of the AG - it is not unusual, however, to hear '4GL' being used as the collective term. Typical front-end tool components are:

- forms systems
- interactive query language
- fourth generation language (4GL)
- 3GL pre-compilers
- report writer
- data dictionary (although likely to be implemented using a back-end DBMS)
- decision support tools
- end user query facilities
- computer aided support environments (analyst workbenches etc).

Back-end

The back-end also consists of a number of elements:

- Database Management System (DBMS) - this supports the physical storage of the data and responds to the control language requests it receives. The DBMS is responsible for maintaining the consistency and integrity of the data, providing necessary programs 'locks' to prevent data being read/updated simultaneously by two or more users and generally ensuring that all problems are overcome

- Distributed Database - this permits the back-end to be distributed across a number of machines. This means that the front-end can access data located on any of the host machines.

Other back-end elements are available for tasks such as the bulk loading of data into the database, for importing to or exporting data from a database, or for recovering the database after a failure. These may collectively form a set of database administrator utilities.

Ideally the back-end elements are transparent to the application and to the application developer. Only the database administrator (DBA) needs to know and understand them. However knowledge of the underlying structure is advantageous to the developer in order to produce an efficient system and to tune it to work effectively.

The front-end need not be on the same hardware as the back-end. Separation of the front-end application processing from the back-end DBMS processing is an essential aspect of distributed processing.

The data control or query language is used by the front-end elements to instruct the back-end elements. The two main elements are:

- data definition language (DDL) - the DDL enables the physical database structure of files, indexes etc to be created and subsequently amended

- data manipulation language (DML) - the DML allows data to be input, to be selected for display, to be updated or to be deleted.

The query language will usually also have the ability to specify security and integrity constraints to be maintained by the DBMS.

ii.3 DBMS architectures

Database Management Systems are categorised by the way their data organisation is visualised and manipulated:

- hierarchical

- network

- inverted list

- relational.

Hierarchical and Network types have until recently been the most widely used types of DBMSs on mainframe computers; relational DBMSs, or RDBMSs, are relative newcomers. In the future, products with support for object oriented concepts are likely to become important.

In recognition of the fact that most evaluations carried out at present are likely to be for RDBMS this volume has adopted relational database terminology.

All DBMSs, however, need to meet the same functional requirements and consequently the criteria in this volume are appropriate for all DBMS evaluations - irrespective of type.

RDBMS

In essence a RDBMS is a collection of two dimensional tables, where a table is data organised into rows and columns. These tables may be joined dynamically through the common values within them. The simplicity of the relational concept of tables makes RDBMSs easier to understand, and so to teach and learn, than other forms of DBMS.

A key feature of RDBMSs is a clear separation of the logical table oriented view of the data from its physical storage, and in particular its indexes. It is not necessary for the programmers, or the end users, to have any knowledge of this physical arrangement.

Manipulation of the data in the tables is by set operators (rather than by record operators). SQL (Structured Query Language) is now generally accepted as the preferred data sublanguage.

The Database Administrator (DBA) is the only person who needs to have knowledge of the physical representation. The DBA is responsible for the mapping between levels.

Hierarchical DBMS

Data in a hierarchic database is logically organised in one or more tree structures.

Hierarchic databases are excellent performers when carrying out transactions that require straightforward tree navigation and where the data is naturally structured in this way. However, whenever an unanticipated query is made that does not fit the rigid tree structure, the searching can become very time consuming. If this type of query is likely to become a common occurrence, then it may be advisable to restructure the database. This is a complex operation requiring specialist skills.

There are some applications for which the data cannot be broken down into a tree structure. In these cases a hierarchic database cannot be implemented.

Network DBMS

Network databases are also known as Navigational or CODASYL systems. The network data structure is an extended form of the hierarchic structure, but with additional cross links between data items. These links are normally implemented within the database by pointers that record the physical placement address of the data, but this dependence can make restructuring difficult.

An extensive network DML in the form of records and links is required to process the data. Typically such a DML works at the record level.

Network DBMSs are inherently complex and the range of operators is large and difficult to learn. Conversely the products are mature, feature rich, and can support a high transaction throughput.

Inverted list

Inverted list products are similar to RDBMS in that the data is stored in tables of columns and rows. The primary difference is that the programmer needs to be aware of the physical storage of the data in order to access it.

Most inverted list vendors have developed relational, usually SQL based, interfaces to their products, thus enabling the benefits of independence, as well as skills portability, to be obtained.

Comparison

The chief advantage of RDBMSs over the older forms of DBMSs is their ease of use and their ability to be changed easily. Change is often required either because of errors in the analysis, or because of changes in the business requirements. RDBMSs offer independence between the application and the logical data, and between the logical data and the physical data storage, thus changes to one do not necessarily affect the others.

Hierarchic and Network databases lack this independence and consequently database restructuring is often very difficult and time consuming. A further drawback to these types of database is that they are poor at handling ad hoc queries.

The relative simplicity of the relational databases makes them easier to modify to run in a distributed environment. The majority of the distributed databases on the market today are based on RDBMS.

Historically the chief limitation of RDBMSs has been their poor performance. This has led to avoidance of RDBMSs where high throughput, or fast response to known transactions, are fundamental requirements. RDBMS products are maturing and are adopting high performance strategies. In addition, with the cost of computer power falling, software performance is becoming less important. For many projects the advantages gained by having the flexibility of an RDBMS may outweigh the drawback of having to buy more powerful hardware to achieve the required performance.

In summary, most data management authorities now accept that in most circumstances the advantages of Relational DBMSs far outweigh the disadvantages. For all but a few performance critical applications a RDBMS will be the natural choice for all DBMS projects.

Several of the older hierarchical or network products have provided relational interfaces to enable them to offer the benefits of relational theory, thereby simplifying the end user interface, but retaining the underlying power (and of course complexity). At the same time the relational products have adopted many ideas from the older products in order to improve their performance.

Introduction ii
Scope

ii.4 Terminology

Products have evolved in different ways, and have consequently adopted different terminologies for features which meet common objectives.

This section describes the terminology adopted in this volume which is offered as one way of finding a generally acceptable data management vocabulary.

The objective of an on-line application is to interact with the user in such a way that the user can efficiently carry out his job. The application will accept data, process and store it, and retrieve it. The user's job might be inputting data, requesting batch processed reports, or obtaining management information on-line by querying the database. The essence of all this is the application requesting input, the user entering it, and then passing it to the computer. We have used the term exchange to refer to this basic 'request, input and send' interaction.

An exchange, therefore, could be any one of the following:

- completion of a data entry form (screen)

- selection of an option from a menu

- cancellation of a help screen

- a single character response to a question, eg 'Accept (Y/N) >'

- in some instances completion of single fields on a form

- direct input of a query language command.

The collection of exchanges into a structure we refer to as the dialogue structure. Typically such a structure will contain menus, forms for data input and query, exchanges which cause reports to be printed or batch operations to be instigated, and often help screens which may be displayed. There will also be a convention as to the means by which the user can leave one exchange and go to another or to a menu, that is generally move about within the dialogue structure provided. This is referred to as navigation.

Processing of the data may be required either before or after an exchange. These are called pre-map and post-map procedures.

iii Criteria

iii.1 Notation

The criteria in this document are structured as a hierarchy, this is illustrated in the annex.

The text is in three classes:

- the main discussion of the criteria - it is primarily this text that should be customised for particular projects against which weights are assigned and scores allotted. To obtain an overview of the criteria this text can be read in isolation. This is printed in 10 point Palatino typeface (ie the one used to print this volume) alongside a numbered heading in bold type, as in the top paragraph on this page. Where the criteria covers a large subject area it is divided into sub-criteria. This is printed in the normal typeface with an unnumbered side heading in the same typeface (ie not bolded)

- detailed discussion of the criteria or sub-criteria - this level is required for information gathering. This is also in the 10 point Palatino typeface, it does not have a heading

- *the supporting questions associated with the criteria or sub-criteria - these are in italics, as this example.*

iii.2 Summary of the criteria

The hierarchy of evaluation criteria against which database management systems can be scored is summarised below and elaborated in the sub-sections which follow. A diagrammatic representation of the hierarchy adopted within this volume appears as an Annex. It will, of course, be necessary to construct a hierarchy applicable to the needs of the project or organisation, which will more than likely be different to the one we have illustrated.

The top level criteria are:

- Data Structure - the capabilities of the data definition and data manipulation languages, together with the ease with which the database structure can be changed to reflect evolving application requirements

- Portability - the extent to which the database definitions, the data, or the skills associated with using the DBMS, are transferable to other environments or products

- Serviceability - the ability of the DBMS to provide a service suitable for the application environment

- Performance - the characteristics of the product in different application environments, including the sophistication of its performance tuning features

- Control and Security - facilities for controlling the development and use of databases

- Data Distribution - the capabilities of the product to support distribution of data across multiple disparate hardware environments

- SSADM Support - the support for SSADM in terms of tools and guidance to aid implementation

- Product Credibility - assessment of the credibility, experience and capability of the product and its vendor

- Access to Potential Technical Developments - the likelihood of the product being able to take advantage of technical developments

- System Development and Productivity tools - comprehensiveness of tools to increase system development productivity which work with the DBMS

- Project Specific Criteria - space for the evaluation team to include any additional requirements

- Costs - assessment of direct and ancillary cost of hardware, software, maintenance and personnel.

It is expected that these criteria, with the exception of costs, will be weighted and scored as set out in the

Overview and Procedures Volume of this library. The cost information will be required as an element of the selection procedure, or to exclude products from detailed consideration when they exceed planned budgets or cost ceilings.

Note that these criteria are not intended to form a tutorial on the subject under consideration. There is a wide range of published material available, including a number of reports and papers from CCTA. Please contact CCTA regarding the availability of appropriate documents.

iii.3 Questions

This annex consists of a discussion of each of the above criteria together with relevant detailed questions.

The questions should be used for familiarisation with a product before attempting to allocate scores against evaluation criteria.

Not all questions are relevant to all products, or projects, and they should be used selectively.

Experience has shown that little will be gained by having the vendor provide written answers to the questions. Only by probing can the evaluation team fully elicit the limits of the capabilities of the products. The best value will be obtained by attempting to answer questions after inspection of technical documentation and attending demonstrations.

1 Data structure and handling

The capabilities of the data definition and manipulation languages, together with the flexibility of the data item constructs, have a major influence on the ease with which applications can be built and maintained. Despite careful analysis and design, there is invariably a need eventually to modify the logical structure of a database. These changes come about because of changing or new requirements. In general, projects should, at present, consider using relational architecture databases unless there are overriding reasons (usually related to high performance or compatibility requirements).

1.1	**Data definition (schema)**	The definition of the logical structure of the data is referred to as the schema. The schema is recorded, for RDBMS, in Schema Information Tables (also known as directories or catalogues, or even, misleadingly, as data dictionaries). The way in which the data is defined has a major effect on the ease with which the structure can be amended. Independence between logical and physical definition, together with the availability of views, ensure that the effect of data structure changes is minimised.
	Logical data structure (schema) definition	The user (developer) view of the data is usually that of the logical data structure. This is often referred to as the schema. Data independence is the decoupling of applications from unnecessary knowledge of the database structure. It is generally recognised that a relational database architecture facilitates a greater degree of data independence than network or hierarchical architecture databases in that applications access data using data values alone. Changes at the physical level, for example to indexes or to placement methods, can be made without impacting the logical view of the data.
		The logical database structure influences the usability of the system. Classifying the DBMS (logical view) as hierarchical, network or relational etc provides a very high level overview as to its general type.
		Is the database logical (schema) structure defined as

- *a collection of hierarchies?*
- *a network structure?*
- *a collection of tables (relations)?*
- *other?*

The schema is created and amended by a data definition language (DDL). These languages differ in form and facilities from DBMS to DBMS.

The relevant international standard for relational products is the SQL (Structured Query Language) standard, ISO 9075:1989, which combines ISO 9075:1987 with the integrity addendum (note that the ANSI equivalent of the old standard - X3.135:1986 - has not, at the time of writing, had the addendum incorporated; they remain separate documents).

A new standard for an enhanced SQL is currently being developed (colloquially known as SQL2), and it is hoped that this upward compatible extension to the ISO 9075 language will become an international standard as soon as possible. Most vendors supply products which have features additional to the existing standard, so caution should be exercised since not all such features will be incorporated into the new standard of SQL.

The corresponding international standard for network databases is the Network Data Language (NDL). CODASYL, while not producing standards have published proposals which have influenced vendors.

Products conforming to a standard provide for easier interchange of data structures, applications and skills. When the definition language is not based on an actual or proposed standard it is important to get the flavour of it to establish its method of operation etc by obtaining examples of its use.

Is the database schema definition language based upon an actual or proposed standard?

If so, which version of which standard and what is the degree of conformance?

Chapter 1
Data structure and handling

To what extent is the vendor committed to making his product conform to developments of the standard?

It is necessary to identify any limits the product imposes on definition of the database structure.

Are there any significant limits applicable when defining the structure (eg number of record types, number of levels within a structure, number of fields within a record, maximum size of records etc)?

Data views (sub-schemas)

Independence between the application program and the logical data is important in that it permits changes to the logical data structure without impacting the application program. In relational DBMSs this may be achieved by accessing the data through a logical subset of data items called a view. In other DBMSs sub-schemas are used. More advanced systems allow a degree of mapping as well as simply sub-setting between the schema and sub-schema data models.

Sub-schemas are necessary for data independence.

Does the DBMS provide facilities for defining application related data views (sub-schemas)?

If so, which (if any) language specific sub-schema data description languages are supported?

Usually, the sub-schema will provide an application data view which is of the same type as the schema view. This is not necessary however.

Is the application data view

- *hierarchical?*
- *a network?*
- *relational?*

Sub-schema capabilities which allow the creation of new entity (record or structure) types provide maximum program data independence. Most sub-schema implementations provide little more than a subsetting capability.

What capabilities in each of the following schema to sub-schema mappings are provided?

- *creation of new structures*
- *creation of sub-schema records by joining schema records*
- *selecting schema records by type*
- *constructing sub-schema records from subsets of the data items in the corresponding schema record*
- *changing data item formats*
- *other.*

It may not be possible to update data in more than one table (type of data record) through a view.

What limitations are there on accessing and updating the underlying data through a view?

Physical database definition	The physical representation of a logical structure affects the performance characteristics of the database. The definition of the database's physical structure, that is storage mechanism, location, compression, clustering, etc, should be separate from the logical schema to allow tuning without impacting applications.

Lack of these facilities inhibits tuning. However, automatic mappings are more usable for small simple systems.

Does the DBMS provide facilities for specifying the physical representation of a logical structure or is the logical to physical mapping automatic?

Is the language used to specify the physical representation integrated into the schema DDL or is it separate?

Some products require physical space to be allocated for storage. This can aid performance, but is also a problem should the space be filled.

Chapter 1
Data structure and handling

Does the product require a reserved area or areas on the hard disk? What happens when such an allocation becomes full?

Note: see also chapter 4.5, 'Performance Tuning Facilities'.

Data item definition

The capabilities of the product in defining data items will affect the type of applications for which the product is suitable. Allowing the user to define his own data types, or subtypes, will simplify application development and will aid data input verification. The ability to associate a data item definition with a set of values (domain) increases the database's understanding of the semantics of the data.

A range of data types are desirable for storage and programming efficiency.

What data types are supported?

Can the user define his own data types or sub-types?

Are domains supported? Can validation rules be attached?

Are null values supported?

For storage efficiency, variable length fields may be desirable. However, not all systems support variable length fields.

Are there any specific restrictions on the use of variable length fields?

Integration (to some degree) of structured data and unstructured data is often desirable, but usually poorly supported.

Are there any provisions for handling unstructured data (eg text or image)?

Data compression may be necessary for storage efficiency.

Do facilities exist to enable data to be compressed?

- *are these provided by the DBMS?*

27

- *are hooks provided for the DBMS to make use of the user's own data compression routines?*

1.2 Data definition (schema) manipulation

During the course of time application requirements alter, thus necessitating changes to the schema (logical tables) in order to reflect the new requirements. This can include adding new columns, changing the definition of existing columns, deleting columns and redefining the relationships between tables. This restructuring of a database frequently involves unloading and then reloading the database. For a large database this is likely to be a very time consuming task. The availability of restructure utilities which are able to make use of the particular arrangement of the internal system structure of the DBMS may be able to accomplish this task rather faster. In any event they may remove the need for writing special purpose restructure applications.

Database restructuring is changing the database logical structure. If the database system exhibits good data independence, programs using data not immediately affected by the restructure should not need changing.

What schema restructuring facilities are available?

Is it necessary to stop the database in order to restructure?

Can indexes be added or renamed?

Can columns be renamed, added, deleted or changed?

Restructure operations often involve unloading, modifying, and then reloading part of the database. It is desirable that utilities exist to facilitate this operation.

Is it necessary to unload the data before restructuring?

What utility programs are provided to facilitate restructuring of a database?

Database reorganisation is the changing of the physical storage mechanisms.

Chapter 1
Data structure and handling

Can the physical storage mechanisms be altered?

Is it necessary to stop the database before reorganisation? Does the data have to be unloaded? What utilities are available to assist with this process?

1.3 Data manipulation

Data in the database is created, altered, queried or deleted by use of a Data Manipulation Language (DML). The DML itself is usually declarative, but it may however include procedural constructs for flow control, or it may be possible to embed it in a 4GL or a 3GL which provides such constructs.

Data manipulation language

Identifies the type of DML.

For record to record processing navigational DMLs are more efficient for predefined retrievals (using existing common DBMS storage architectures) than set based (relational) DMLs. However, set based DMLs are easier to use, are more suitable for non expert users, and usually allow greater program data (structure) independence.

Is the DML navigational (ie record at a time, exploiting links between records) or is it set based (relational)?

'Host language' DMLs interface to conventional programming languages. The adoption of a self contained interactive DML will require some educational overhead for programmers (which may be quite small). It is also likely to have an impact on the installation's standards and procedures.

Can the DML for the DBMS be used interactively? Can it be embedded in a host language?

Investigate the extent of the facilities offered by the DML

What commands exist within the DML? To what extent does the DML comply with international standards? What extensions does it contain and to what extent do they comply with draft standards?

29

Self contained DMLs usually only support a restricted set of data types. Escaping into a conventional programming language may provide a method of interfacing to existing files. Also, many self contained DMLs are interpreted, and therefore not particularly efficient for serious computation.

Can conventional language subroutines be invoked from the self contained DML?

Are DML commands interpreted or compiled?

Access to conventional files is frequently necessary for data interchange. The facility may be provided by DML primitives or by using CALLed routines written in a conventional programming language.

Can the self contained DML also access conventional files?

The ability to construct DML commands dynamically at run time may be beneficial.

Is dynamic DML supported?

Record selection capabilities	The record selection capabilities of the DML have a major influence on the ease with which an application can be written.

Data is accessed through a data item, or a group of data items, known as the key.

While predefined keys are usually the most efficient, the ability to access records without predefining the keys in the schema is useful for ad hoc and one off applications

Can database searches only be undertaken using predefined keys?

Can boolean search criteria be stipulated? What limits are there on the complexity of the search criteria?

Can nested selection be implemented?

Restricting keys to a single data item may limit or constrain the placement of data within records.

Can a key be a combination of data items?

Chapter 1
Data structure and handling

Can a predefined key be a combination of data items?

Serial access is usually the most efficient for batch 'scanning' type applications. Generic or partial key searching is occasionally necessary.

Can records be accessed serially, in physical address sequence?

Are there positional capabilities (next/ prior/ first/ last/ Nth)?

Is the relational concept of 'cursors' supported? Can multiple cursors be active?

Not all systems allow duplicate key values; to handle such keys, the DML, if navigational, requires a 'fetch next record with duplicate key value' verb.

Are duplicate keys allowed, or must all records have a unique key?

Are there any specific restrictions on the handling of duplicated key values?

Embedded data manipulation language	The DML often needs to be supplemented by a 3rd or 4th generation programming language. Languages supported should include those normally used by the installation. Alternatively the DML itself might have additional processing functionality.

Which host languages are supported?

Does the DML include flow control and processing constructs?

DML calls expressed as extensions to a host language are more readable and easier to use than CALL type statements. They do however require either compiler extensions, or more usually, a preprocessor to convert the language extensions down to CALL statements. The parameters of such CALL statements may be encoded and not directly intelligible.

Are DML commands normally expressed as CALL statements or as extensions to the host language?

Are these commands implemented using an extended compiler or using a preprocessor?

Investigate the extent of non DML (ie 4GL) capabilities. In particular, where there is not the (direct) power of a host language, then the following facilities should be available:

- processing non database files (for inter system data interchange)

- data reformatting (if DBMS is not rich in data types)

- ability to call conventional language subroutines to handle exceptions or for performance reasons.

- error handling.

What other capabilities are provided within the language under the following categories?

- *Arithmetic*

- *String and Text handling*

- *Conditional processing*

- *Terminal handling*

- *Printing and reporting*

- *Other.*

Stored DML

Business logic may be coded using DML commands and stored in tables managed by the DBMS. These 'rules' may then be triggered by the occurrence of certain specified conditions. Storing such rules at the DBMS ensures that such logic cannot be contravened by the applications, makes it easier to maintain, and can aid performance. Inter table validation and referential actions may usefully be implemented using such facilities.

Can DML statements or 'procedures' be held in the database?

Chapter 1
Data structure and handling

How are these triggered?

Are there restrictions on the commands that may be used or what can be accomplished?

Are these held in compiled form, that is with the execution plan predefined?

2 Portability

Portability as a strategic objective for database systems can be considered at several levels. These include portability of the DBMS product, of the data definition (schema), of the data, and of the skills of the applications developers.

2.1 DBMS portability

It is necessary to establish what particular environments are supported. Lists of operating systems and transaction processing monitors may not be particularly meaningful, as not every transaction processing monitor will operate under every operating system.

On what machine/operating system/transaction processing monitor combinations does the product run?

Products often take advantage of specific features of an environment. These features may not be available on another system.

Does the DBMS take advantage of specific features of the environment? Does the data sublanguage (DDL and DML) differ between environments?

2.2 Schema portability

It may be necessary to be able to re-implement the database using a different DBMS, adherence to standards aids such portability.

If the database definition language is based upon an actual or proposed international standard, which standard and what is the degree of conformance?

2.3 Data portability

Adoption of multiple database management systems based on the same database architecture and standard (for example SQL) usually allows data to be ported between sites with few problems. Unless the system software and database environments are identical, porting of data will invariably involve a database unload/reload operation. Factors such as implementor specific character sets or collating sequences can cause very severe problems.

What mechanisms are available for exporting/importing data?

Do the different environments on which the DBMS is supported have common character sets/collating sequences etc?

2.4 Skill mobility

Application skill mobility between sites (if required) will be maximised if a common system and application environment is chosen. Adoption of a common database architecture (such as SQL) will enable application programmers to move between differing database environments with reduced retraining costs, especially if application development is undertaken using 3GL tools. However, if a 4GL development environment is chosen then it is likely that its standardisation will affect staff mobility more significantly. Many of the more advanced 4GL tools make the choice of DBMS transparent to the application programmer and so in such environments, the choice of DBMS does not affect skill mobility.

To what extent does the product support skill mobility?

3 Serviceability

Serviceability relates to the ability of the DBMS to provide suitable service, to maintain the integrity of the data, and, in particular, be resilient to hardware or software malfunction.

3.1 Multi user capabilities

It is important that the DBMS adequately supports suitable levels of concurrent usage. For small application environments this may be simply be a question of asking whether the DBMS supports multiple concurrent users.

If the DBMS is to support concurrent usage then it needs to ensure that there are no problems arising from data contention (covered by 3.4 Integrity below). The number of users that a DBMS can support may be limited by any one of a number of factors.

Is there a limit on the number of concurrent users? What are the limiting factors and how do they affect the maximum?

To establish data storage and memory resources required. In a (shared) service environment many aspects must be considered, there is probably a storage requirement for the service plus individual storage requirements for each user. Also, storage for buffers etc may be variable, but a realistic amount is required.

What is the main storage requirement for the DBMS to support (note that this should exclude the requirements of the application that should be separately assessed):

- *on-line applications?*

- *batch applications?*

Can the DBMS support shared (update) access to data

- *by on-line application programs?*

- *by batch application programs?*

- *by concurrent batch and on-line applications?*

Products can run out of memory when more than a handful of users try to access the system, so techniques such as multi threading are often used to overcome this.

Is there a recommended minimum amount of machine resource that should be allowed for each concurrent user?

3.2 Recovery

On-line updating of data in a multi user environment requires that the mechanisms within the DBMS provide the ability to recover from any form of failure. This invariably requires that log files have to be used to keep a record of all actions that have changed the data.

Recovery may be addressed from two viewpoints:

a) the mechanisms available in the product for backup and restore, logging, rollback, authorisation and automation

b) how the product deals with a specific form of failure; of the application, media, etc

Criteria are provided below for both viewpoints. In an evaluation one should be chosen for weighting and scoring - the other may then be used to gain further insights into the capability of the products.

a) Mechanisms

Backup and restore

Dumping the whole database produces a self consistent copy, but may not be practical for large databases. If selected parts only are dumped, care must be taken to ensure that dumped and undumped parts are restored to a common consistent state.

What forms of database dumping are allowed:

- *whole database?*

- *selected parts of the database?*

Database backups may either be taken as an image of the disk, or a backup of the data files. The former is usually quicker, but offers less control when carrying out a restore.

Chapter 3
Serviceability

What types of database archive can be taken:

- *image dump?*
- *data backup?*

Systems requiring constant availability may necessitate dumping (part of) the database while applications are still processing it. This means that the dumped portion is not necessarily self consistent. When restored, the DB system log/journal must be processed to roll forward those records changed between the time they were dumped and the end of the dumping operation.

Can the database be dumped while applications are active? If so, how is consistency maintained?

Updates to volatile data are likely to cause a number of entries on the log. For recovery purposes, only the most recent entry may be relevant. It is useful to have a utility that deletes all except the most recent entry. Similarly, recovering from an unprocessed log results in random updates across the target files. Sorting the entries into address sequence minimises head movement time.

Are utilities available to compress/reorder log information for efficient reprocessing when restoring and rolling forward a database?

Logs

In order to return the database to a consistent up to date state following failure and restoration of the backup it is essential to have 'logs' (or journals) available to 'roll forward' the database.

What form of logs are held to enable database roll forward:

- *transaction logs?*
- *after image logs?*

If after image logs are maintained do they contain:

- *images of the data pages?*
- *images of the data records?*

39

- *images of the data items?*

In certain circumstances, for example when loading data in a batch, it may not be appropriate to log changes to the indexes.

Are index changes logged? Can this facility be switched off? Does the DBMS contain facilities to rebuild indexes?

Maintaining more, smaller, logs can benefit recovery.

Are logs maintained separately by database, by table, or by user?

Dual logs may be required for resilience. Operating without logs may be useful for special processes such as loading or some batch runs.

What non standard journalising and logging options are provided?

- *dual logs*
- *operating without logs.*

Some systems require specific device types (eg tapes) for logging.

What device types are required for logs and journals?

If DBMS log files can be processed for audit, analysis, or accounting purposes, it may be desirable for an application to write a record to the log for later processing.

Can applications write information to logs for audit or other purposes?

The order in which operations are written to the logs will affect the extent to which recovery may be accomplished.

In what order is information written to the logs? How does this affect recovery?

Rollback

The DBMS must have a strategy for removing, or 'rolling back', the effects of incorrect or incomplete success units (the logical amount of work performed by an application that moves the database content from one self consistent state to another self consistent state). This is usually accomplished either by recording the state of the data before update, that is 'before images', or by not physically writing any data until the success unit has been successfully completed ('delayed update' or 'group commit').

What strategy is used for ensuring that incomplete or incorrect transactions can be rolled back?

Before images are usually only held until the transaction has been completed, in which case they are not necessarily stored on disc. Storing images may affect performance adversely.

Are before image logs maintained?

Authority

It may be a requirement that database level recovery be initiated only by persons with 'database administrator' authority. Applications should be able to roll back their own updates to the last (application defined) success unit boundary or checkpoint.

What level of database recovery can be initiated

- *by the operator?*
- *by an application?*
- *by another means (please specify)?*

Automation

Automatic recovery, on service initiation, makes for operational simplicity. The term 'synchronisation point' (synchpoint) is used to represent a boundary point between two consecutive transactions and equates loosely to the end of a logical unit of work.

After a system failure is recovery of all affected databases to their latest synchpoint automatic?

If database recovery is likely to involve multiple archives, possibly of different parts of the database, and many logs, then intelligent system support is beneficial.

What support does the system provide to enable the database to be restored efficiently?

Automatic recovery may not always be useful, especially if the error is minor and known, and if the recovery is lengthy.

Are there any circumstances when database recovery is automatic, for example upon certain error conditions being detected? Can this feature be turned off?

b) Failure Modes

On-line application failure

In an on-line environment a transaction can be terminated for several reasons. If the transacation fails without notice, then all data changes for that transaction must be aborted and the database 'rolled back' to its last consistent state. If the DBMS fails (perhaps because of a deadlock), then the changes must be 'rolled back' to its last consistent state and the transaction automatically reapplied.

What happens if an on-line transaction fails to complete?

In an on-line environment, it is necessary for there to be a degree of coordination between DBMS, TP and operating system recovery, so that if a transaction is aborted, any database changes are rolled back.

Is database backup and recovery integrated with TP/operating system recovery?

Batch application failure

While logically a batch may comprise a number of small success units, frequently these are artificially grouped into larger units for performance reasons. In some instances batch applications are best run with logging disabled, with a database backup being taken at the end of the run.

What facilities are available for logging batch applications and what happens should the application fail?

Media failure

If database media failure is discovered when reading or writing data it may be possible to circumvent the damaged media or the database may have to be stopped and a recovery instigated.

Chapter 3
Serviceability

What happens if the DBMS discovers a media failure? Is the intervention of an operator called for?

Failure of the logging media is often not detected until it is required in a recovery. The only safeguards are to run duplex logs, or to make backup copies of all logs.

Are any utilities available to overcome corruption of the logging media?

Processor or system software failure

Processor or system software failure usually means that the DBMS loses control with the database being left in an indeterminate state. A mixture of roll forward and roll back will be required.

How does the DBMS recover from a processor or system software failure?

Handling of conventional files

Conventional files are frequently used for print files or for communication with other systems. Some DBMS systems do not reposition such files when the database is recovered. This is especially significant in a TP environment, where on-line transactions interact with the database and then produce printed output.

When an application is restarted does database recovery include repositioning of conventional files?

3.3 Resilience

If uninterrupted operation is important, then duplexing of data and journals as an insurance against media failure may be important. Also, some database products require periodic house keeping runs (for instance to consolidate fragmented dead space or to tidy indexes).

Dualling may be necessary for systems demanding constant availability. It implies maintaining multiple copies (usually two) of selected parts of the database. If one copy becomes unavailable because of media failure, the system continues with the other. The DBMS must also be capable of resynchronising the copies when the failed copy becomes available again.

Can critical parts of a database be dualled?

Even if uninterrupted running is not a requirement, recovery times may vary significantly according to the sophistication of the DBMS's recovery mechanisms.

Are regular periodic housekeeping runs required? If so, can they be run whilst the application is running?

How long do the housekeeping procedures take to run?

3.4 Integrity

The term integrity is used in database contexts with the meaning of accuracy, correctness, or validity. The object is to guard the database against invalid updates. Invalid updates can be caused by errors in data entry, by mistakes on the part of the operator or the application program, or by system failure. A database is said to be in a consistent state when all items in the database that should be in agreement with or compatible with each other are in such a state.

Data integrity is maintained both by ensuring that the data is in a consistent state as input by the users, but also by ensuring that such input complies with restraints defined in the specification. Some relational systems include the ability to define integrity constraints that will be validated automatically by the DBMS. Such facilities are considered by many data processing professionals to be essential in a shared data environment as applications cannot be trusted to maintain the data integrity of the database. However such facilities are usually expensive in terms of their machine usage. The current SQL Standard includes an integrity enhancement feature, therefore most SQL conforming relational products are likely to include this facility eventually.

Database integrity checking

Within any database of significant size a policing/audit role is required to inspect the data and control information to ensure its correctness.

The structural integrity of the database can only be validated using system software (as application programs do not have access to the necessary information). Some vendors provide utility programs for this purpose.

Chapter 3
Serviceability

What software is available to validate

- *the structural integrity of the database (ie pointers and control information for non relational products)?*

- *the data integrity of the database (ie data values and the relationships existing between them)?*

To correct non data errors, some vendors provide diagnostic and fixing utilities. The use of such facilities should be restricted to database administration staff only.

In the event of an error being detected are facilities available to correct the error?

Data Integrity

Correct application programs transform the database from one self consistent state to another. While the application is operating, the database may be inconsistent. As the definition of self consistency depends upon the semantics of the application, only the application can specify when it considers the database self consistent.

Success units depend on application semantics, and must therefore be defined within the application.

Can application programs indicate database success unit boundaries (synchpoints)?

If an application fails, it has not completed its current success unit, the database must therefore be assumed to be inconsistent. Automatic backout ensures the database is returned to a consistent state.

If an application fails is it automatically backed out to its latest application synchpoint?

Application initiated rollback without cancelling the application is a useful facility. Frequently an application is able to detect that it cannot proceed, but also needs to terminate tidily.

Can an application specifically request that database updates are rolled back to the last database synchpoint with the application program remaining active?

45

With multiple applications active, success unit durations will overlap. Therefore, while the database subsets used by individual applications will be self consistent, the database as a whole will not be. If it is desired to be able to say that the database is consistent at a particular time, an operator capability is required.

In a shared service environment can the operator indicate either application specific or system wide synchpoints?

Note that in addition to application synchpoints (success unit boundaries), modern DBMSs have their own checkpoints (consistency points or synchpoints). It is at these points in time that the DBMS writes updates to disk, and ensures that the database is consistent across all applications. The interval between these checkpoints should be a tuning option.

Does the database writer use the concept of 'checkpoints'?

How is the 'checkpoint' interval specified:?

- *a number of transactions*
- *a time interval*
- *a combination of the above*
- *other.*

Is the 'checkpoint' interval tunable by the DBA?

Data validation

It is valuable to be able to record data validation rules with the database to ensure that all applications adhere to them.

Can data validation rules be held along with the data definition and be enforced at runtime? What limits are there to the sophistication of such validation rules?

Database procedures may be used to validate the integrity of data. Similarly, under some circumstances, it may be desirable to derive data when it is required rather than just reading it from the database.

Do facilities exist to enable the specification of database procedures, to be invoked automatically (triggered) on data

Chapter 3
Serviceability

access and storage? If so, can these procedures access database data?

Referential integrity

In many applications there is a specific defined relationship between items of data in two or more files (or tables) for example in an order processing system between orders and order lines. Specific integrity rules between such files must be maintained; for example, the rule for deletion could be that deletion of an order be prevented if there are any order lines in the appropriate table, or it could be that when an order is deleted all associated order lines are removed in a cascade delete. The definition and enforcement of these rules is called referential integrity.

Many products only allow referential integrity to be implemented within the application. This can result in inconsistent implementation and can be a major problem where the referential integrity rules are subject to change. It is preferable for the referential integrity rules to be maintained centrally by the DBMS.

Does the DBMS support referential integrity?

The two main approaches to implementing referential integrity in the DBMS are either to define the rules in the form of DML procedures, which are then triggered, or to extend the data item definition to include the necessary constraints. In either case there could be a performance overhead, although this would probably be less than if the referential integrity had been implemented in the application.

If the DBMS supports referential integrity how is this achieved and what is the effect on performance?

Shared service data integrity

When multiple applications are operating concurrently, their success units must not interfere with each other. Two approaches are possible:

- predefine what resources are required, and suspend the application's initiation until they are available

47

- allow applications to run concurrently and handle any contention if (and when) it arises.

Predefining the resources required is the most efficient (processing) method of handling shared concurrent access to data. Protected modes allow other run units to access the data but not to update it.

Which of the following modes of use can an application declare when opening (part of) a database?

- *exclusive update*
- *protected update*
- *non protected update*
- *exclusive retrieval*
- *protected retrieval*
- *non protected retrieval.*

Alternatively a product may utilise 'optimistic locking' whereby it is assumed that it is less expensive to deal with any contentions that occur than to maintain locks.

Does the product support 'optimistic' locking? If so how are contentions handled? Can the use of 'optimistic locking' be selective, ie by table?

To maximise data sharing, the unit of locking (granularity) should be small. However, this imposes significant performance and resource overheads, so usually some form of compromise is used - typically locking at the DBMS unit of transfer level (block or page). Ideally, the unit of locking should be a tuning parameter.

At what level of granularity can the DBMS lock units of the database to avoid update contention?

- *entire database*
- *realm or area*
- *file*

- *table*
- *block or page*
- *record*
- *item*
- *other.*

For efficiency the record of the locks held must be kept in memory, thus limiting the maximum number that can be held. If the limit is reached then the options are either to delay transactions until there is space in memory to hold the necessary locks, or to raise temporarily the level of granularity of the locking.

Is there a maximum number of locks that can be held at any one time? What happens if the maximum is reached?

Some hardware has sophisticated lock mechanisms that provide benefits that DBMSs cannot match. Use of these may affect application portability.

Does the product maintain locks itself or does it rely on a lock manager provided by the underlying operating system and hardware?

What are the advantages and disadvantages of the approach taken?

Unless an application predeclares which resources it will use, it is possible for deadlock between two or more transactions to occur. If this happens, the DBMS usually rolls back one of the transactions to its previous success unit boundary. In a batch environment the program will usually be informed that the deadlock has occurred.

How does the DBMS detect deadlocks?

What action does the DBMS take when a deadlock occurs?

Chapter 4
Performance

4 Performance

Traditionally, relational database systems have been associated with information systems and only network and hierarchical products with high throughput transaction systems. This reflected the performance characteristics of the relatively primitive architectures of early relational systems. More recently, increased sophistication of RDBMS products and cheaper processing power has increased the scope to use relational systems for larger databases and higher throughput systems. However, performance and the ability to tune a database system are still very significant factors for high throughput systems and most relational database vendors are addressing this topic by increasing the sophistication of their query processors, precompiling DML statements and adding more sophisticated data accessing mechanisms.

Whilst performance is likely to remain an issue for a few years yet it is now true to say that many relational products can now supply performance to match all but the most onerous transaction processing (TP) tasks.

4.1 Characteristics for management information systems

MIS are characterised by having relatively low transaction rates, but high ad hoc query rates. Essential to efficient use is a good query optimiser. A query optimiser analyses queries and attempts to devise the most efficient way (in machine resource terms) of executing that query.

What are the major features of the query optimiser? What factors are taken into account?

The quality of the query optimiser is limited by the information about the content of the database available to it.

Is there a utility to provide statistics about the content of the database for the query optimiser?

Do the available statistics include information about the distribution of values within the database?

One potential problem is that, possibly inadvertently, an onerous query could swamp the system resources.

Is there any form of 'governor' or similar mechanism to avoid individual queries utilising excessive machine resource?

4.2 Characteristics for on-line TP systems

Data access in an on-line transaction processing environment usually involves high transaction rates, but with each transaction only accessing a small number of data records. Such accesses, using indexes, are likely to be reasonably efficient for most reputable relational database products. However, many of those products have evolved from a minicomputer background and are not designed to operate in a TP monitor hosted environment.

The use of a TP monitor in an on-line environment, besides providing system control functionality, tends to reduce system overheads, in particular those associated with main storage and process management, and communications.

Is the product designed to operate in a TP environment? If so, which TP monitors can it use?

Recent releases of products are including many, sometimes optional, performance enhancements. These include precompilation of DML statements, client / server architecture, stored procedures, multi server architectures, multi threading, external cache use, etc.

Does the product have any specific features which improve performance in an on-line transaction processing environment?

Vendors are now often happy to supply benchmarks of their product(s) running standards such as TP1, or 'debit credit'. These should be used with caution since there are many variables which can be 'adjusted' to attain performance never achievable in practise.

Can the vendor supply reports of independently verified industry standard benchmarks?

Chapter 4
Performance

4.3 Characteristics for batch systems

Batch applications usually process large volumes of data, frequently involving high hit rates on database data. System overheads caused by the processing of complex DML statements or structurally complex data may result in unacceptably long run times and may be rectifiable only at the expense of compromising the logical integrity of the data structure. It is in a batch environment that optimisation such as precompiling of DML statements is likely to be of particular importance.

The usual options are use of a 3GL or a report writer. The ability to sort the data prior to submission to the DBMS often brings performance benefits.

How can the product be used to build efficient and effective batch systems?

4.4 Characteristics for mixed systems

Many systems will have a mix of MIS, on-line TP, and batch processing. For these it will be necessary to implement some form of prioritisation, perhaps to ensure that the chief executive gets a good response time, or to ensure that the on-line TP throughput is not affected by batch runs or complex queries.

Does the product have any features which enable priorities to be allocated to specific users or processes, or groups thereof?

Can batch runs or enquiries be run in background?

4.5 Tuning facilities

Regardless of the effort put in to physical database design, variations in application profiles will necessitate changes to the physical structure to tune performance. The DBMS must provide facilities to enable monitoring of the database's performance. Subsequently, the DBA is likely to want to tune the storage structure by a reorganisation, using for example, additional indexes or alternative storage mechanisms. An advanced DBMS will provide a number of such storage mechanisms. With the current state of technology it is unlikely that reorganisations on large databases can be achieved without an interruption to the database service.

| Physical structure representation | The methods available for physical storage will have a major influence on performance. |

Control over the placement of data allows the database to be designed and tuned to suit performance requirements. Briefly, the different placement methods provide the following capabilities:

- general hashing - good default; efficient key based retrieval; no concept of key ordering without an extract and sort or some additional structuring

- constrained hashing - as general hashing, but may be more efficient to extract records for sorting etc

- clustering - provides efficient access to groups of related records

- displaced clustering - as clustering, but can avoid contention between multiple clusters

- sequential - good for ordered retrieval; frequently causes problems with overflow on insertion

- B-tree - an efficient dynamic indexing method which contains all keys within the data set

- ISAM - indexed sequential file accessing method.

Which of the following techniques may be used to determine a record's placement within the database?

- *hashing or randomising to anywhere in the database*

- *using a hashing or randomising technique, but with placement constrained to a subsection of the database*

- *clustered near a specific (owner) record*

- *clustered, but at a displacement from a specific (owner) record*

- *direct (application determined address)*

- *sequential*

Chapter 4
Performance

- *B-tree*
- *ISAM*
- *other*.

Data in relational tables may be accessed via either the primary or secondary keys and tables joined when required by matching values. Other types of DBMS have different mechanisms for relating records which have different performance characteristics. A choice of such mechanisms allows the database administrator to tune the database structure. Briefly, the different methods for representing relationships exhibit the following characteristics:

- ordered indexes - allows efficient keyed random access to members of a relation. Especially suited to relationships with a large number of members

- unordered indexes - efficient for relationships where the major part of processing is serial through the relationships members. Does not efficiently support key ordered relationships

- physical contiguity - efficient for static relationships

- correspondence between data items - flexible, but needs indexes to access members if sets are large

- unidirectional pointers - often referred to as a 'forward chains'. Best where majority of processing is in the forward direction. Possible poor performance when removing member records from a relation as this requires locating the prior member

- bidirectional pointers - provides for efficient removal of member records, but involves a space overhead. Is also less efficient when inserting members into the relation.

What mechanisms may be used to represent logical relationships existing between records?

- *ordered indexes (sort keys)*

- *unordered indexes (pointer arrays)*
- *physical contiguity*
- *correspondence between data items values*
- *unidirectional pointers*
- *bidirectional pointers*
- *other (please specify)*.

The indexes to the keys of relational tables may be stored using the same placement techniques as for data storage. For other types of database there are options for performance tuning when retrieving data. Briefly, the following characteristics may be provided:

- hashing - efficient, but only allows for a single key. Does not allow access by generic key or by sort sequence

- direct - efficient, using the record real address. Useful for relocating a record quickly within a run unit. Not recommended as an access technique when this would involve saving the record address between run units

- single indexes - usually less efficient than hashing, but allows generic key or sort sequence accessing

- multiple indexes - as for single indexes, but also provides for secondary indexes to data. Possible performance implications when adding data. The omission of multiple indexing capabilities usually necessitates artificial structures within the schema.

What mechanisms may be specified to facilitate efficient retrieval of data?

- *hashing or randomising*
- *direct (record) addressing*
- *single indexes to a record*

Chapter 4
Performance

- *multiple indexes to a record*
- *other.*

Monitoring and statistics

Statistics are required to help the database administrator decide when to reorganise and to help programmers and operators monitor their respective applications and systems.

Information of use to the DBA would include:

- percentage of free space available

- percentage of records not in their home (as defined by the placement criteria) block or page

- depth of indexes

- access profiles etc.

What statistics are available to the DBA to advise him when to reorganise the database?

Programmers require statistics to monitor the execution of their programs. Examples include:

- number of DML calls (of each type)

- whether deadlock occurred.

What statistics are available to programmers during or after a program execution?

Operators require statistics to operate a service satisfactorily. Some of these statistics may be associated with the operating system rather than the DBMS specifically. Examples of DBMS specific statistics include:

- free space remaining on the log file(s)

- number of run units suspended, awaiting DB resources.

What statistics are available to the operator when running in a shared service environment?

57

For peak performance the statistics should include data about distribution of values within a database table. Frequency of update of these statistics should be related to the rate of change of the database.

What statistics are used by the database query optimiser? How are such statistics updated?

Reorganisation

Changing the database physical structure, without altering the logical structure, is necessary to continue to meet performance requirements in a changing environment.

The more flexibility provided, the more options the database administrator has for tuning the database. Principal options include:

- changing a record's placement mode

- changing clustering controls

- changing placement of files or datasets

- changing the way in which relationships are represented etc.

To what extent is it possible to alter the physical structure of the database (for performance reasons) without affecting the logical structure or the applications?

Reorganisation is a time consuming process. It is desirable to be able to undertake this while the database is active. Few if any DBMSs provide this capability.

Can this reorganisation be undertaken while applications are using the database?

Utilities are probably required to unload and reload the parts of the database. If the storage architecture is pointer based, these utilities will need to update pointers to reorganised records.

What utilities are available to facilitate off-line database reorganisation?

Some DBMSs do not reclaim space from deleted records or index entries. With such systems, this space is reclaimed with special reorganisation utility runs.

Under what circumstances is a database reorganisation necessary (rather than desirable for performance reasons)?

Query Tuning

Unfortunately it is a characteristic of most products that execution performance of a query is affected by the way in which the query is structured, as well as the way in which the data and indexes are held.

Are there better, and worse, ways of writing particular types of queries? Does the product, or the vendor, offer guidance on tuning queries?

Skill Levels

The range of tuning options, the combination of which can result in an almost infinite number of ways of running a system, provides the DBA with enormous flexibility. Their successful manipulation, however, necessitates a high level of practical skill with the product - a skill which rapidly dates as the product is enhanced.

What tuning skills are required? How may they be obtained and maintained? What support does the vendor offer?

4.6 Recovery performance

In many environments the performance of the recovery system is an important criteria. This can only realistically be assessed against the particular requirements of the organisation.

How long does it take to back up the database, or specific portions of the database?

In the event of a failure how long will it take to restore the database, or a specific portion, and roll it forward using the logs?

It may be possible to tune for improved recovery performance, although doing this is likely to impact the throughput achievable by the DBMS.

Are there tuning facilities which affect recovery performance - for example database checkpoint intervals, or size and number of logs?

5 Control and security

For all non trivial systems it is important to control the development and operation of the system, and the structure and content of the database. Such control depends on the facilities provided by the DBMS and on its integration with associated development tools.

5.1 Ownership

Databases must have been created, the person who did this is the 'owner' (DBO) and may consequently have special rights over the database. Databases also need to be administered and in general this requires a Database Administrator (DBA).

Control over who can do what with a database, both for the end users and system developers, will be vested in an individual, usually the DBO or the DBA.

Who controls the database? Can this individual delegate his authority or elements of it?

5.2 Operational controls

The ability to isolate sections of the database for maintenance purposes and subsequently reinstate them, preferably without interrupting the service on other sections of the database may be desirable. The provision of monitoring statistics is necessary for the database administrator to predict when sections of the database are likely to become full or when performance is likely to degrade.

Can sections of the database be isolated for backup or reorganisation? Can other parts of the database be used concurrently?

What facilities are available to alert the DBA that maintenance is required?

5.3 Control over access to data

Shared databases are likely to contain data which is not updatable by certain classes of users. If a database is to contain confidential data then access to such data may also be forbidden. Commonly provided access control facilities include the ability to define user groups (to allocate common privileges to them), the ability to control specific classes of command (such as update commands) and the ability to hide tables or columns from view. Some database systems also provide for access control of occurrences of rows in tables and some data may require audit facilities to record who has accessed it.

Access controls may initially be restricted (ie the default being not to allow access and the access control being set to permit access) or they may be restrictive. Restrictive access controls are more common. Note, DBMS-provided facilities to control access at occurrence (record or data item) level is rare; if provided, it is usually implemented using DBA-specified database procedures. Access control should supplement the operating system facilities, not supplant them.

What access control facilities are provided for

- *the entire database?*

- *major logical sections of the database (eg realms, tables or files)?*

- *data views or subschemas?*

- *tables (record types)?*

- *domains (data item types)?*

- *rows (record occurrences)?*

- *columns (data item occurrences)?*

- *the use of programs or transaction types?*

- *the use of specific DML or DDL commands?*

- *other?*

Can the restrictions or privileges be assigned to groups of users, or only to individual users?

Procedures can be made more sophisticated than simple passwords. Access to data within the database by such procedures, while desirable, is rare.

Are access controls confined to simple passwords or can the DBA-specified procedures be invoked to validate user passwords? Can these procedures access data within the database?

In a controlled environment, attempted access control violations should at least be logged. In a secure environment, it may be necessary to inform the DBA and to disconnect the user's terminal.

What action is taken by the DBMS on an attempted access control violation?

The DBMS should log all database activity. Processing the audit trail can provide information regarding access patterns, performance characteristics and attempted security violations.

What information can the DBMS log to provide an audit trail of database activity?

What facilities can be used to query logs of use, attempted security and other violations?

5.4 Development control

The best way of achieving controlled development of an application is by use of a data dictionary system or repository. The following sub criteria are only applicable in the event of a development data dictionary not being available or where the site does not plan to use one. In this case the database definition will be held in the internal Schema Information Tables (catalogue or directory).

Version control

Development will usually progress through several versions. Even when the application is in use there will probably need to be new versions under development in parallel with the production version. Note that there often is a need for separate development and production hardware.

How can separate versions of the database be maintained?

Configuration management

Configuration management is essential to provide four basic functions:

- unique identification of all data products used in the development

- support the for change control process
- give management visibility into progress and statistics
- support the production of baseline releases.

What configuration management facilities are provided by the product?

Documentation

The definition of the database, along with any changes in the structure or use of the database, needs to be documented. If such documentation is a by product of a separate data dictionary keeping it in step with changes may be a problem and bridging software may be required.

Easy to use means of producing documentation are vital.

What facilities are available for documenting the database definition, integrity constraints, and access privileges?

5.5 Security

CCTA advocate use of CRAMM - the CCTA Risk Analysis and Management Methodology, as an element of the planning for Information Systems. CRAMM reviews the requirements for security, including those associated with use of a DBMS, in a more systematic manner than can be included in this document. A CRAMM study will indicate a number of measures which can be used to draw up criteria and questions, appropriate to the particular requirement, for inclusion here in the evaluation model.

6 Data distribution

There is a growing awareness of the need within an organisation to link together the data available on multiple sites and in multiple DBMSs to form a corporate whole. This information resource can then be made available to all employees of the organisation.

Please note that this chapter does not provide fully detailed criteria for evaluation of distributed database products. Organisations will need to expand on this in the light of their requirements. In particular they should be aware that distribution makes many other requirements more difficult to achieve; for example serviceability and security require special attention.

6.1 Distributed processing

With distributed processing the front-end elements of the DBMS, together with the application development tools, can be located on machine A separately from the back-end data manager on machine B. The user can then switch from using the back-end on machine B, to using one on machine C. By implication the user is aware of the distribution.

Can the user terminal be attached to a different machine than that on which the data resides?

Can the user switch to a different database on a different machine accessed across a network?

Can the application run on a different machine from that which stores the data?

6.2 Distributed database

A distributed database is one in which the data, whilst forming a single logical unit, is in fact distributed, over multiple sites, across multiple DBMSs, or both. Where multiple sites are involved they will be networked together, either through local area networks (LANs) or networks covering large distances. The distributed database may be considered to be the union of a set of local autonomous databases.

Distributed databases may either be homogeneous, ie all the hardware and DBMS software are the same, or heterogeneous, where they are dissimilar. Where there are different products that all conform to the SQL standard the system may be considered homogeneous.

There are a number of issues relating to distributed databases which, distributed relational database theorists say are necessary, but in fact may not actually be required by all projects. In fact some projects may specifically not want them. These are described in the criteria below.

Transparency

Essential to distributed databases theory is that the function of such systems be totally transparent to the users and to the application. Applications built to run on a single machine should be capable of being distributed without changes. The existing front-end should be able to talk to the distributed data manager (DDM) in exactly the same way as it did to the previous back-end before distribution. The DDM should understand and handle all the distributed implications. This implies:

- location transparency - no need to know where the data is stored

- replication transparency - the existence of (for security or performance reasons), and maintenance of, copies of data should be hidden

- fragmentation transparency - the horizontal and vertical slicing of the data by row and/or column, and distribution of the fragments, should be hidden

- transaction transparency - users need not know what actually happens when transactions update their database tables

- system transparency - users need not know the details of hardware, networks, operating system etc.

The transparency must not extend to the distributed database administrator. The DDBA must know what is happening in order to tune the system.

Chapter 6
Data distribution

Currently products do little to meet the objectives of transparency. It should be recognised that transparency is contrary to the concept of ownership, where users wish to 'own', and control, their data.

To what extent does the distributed database product meet the objectives of transparency?

Performance

A major benefit of distributed database is that it permits incremental growth, which can be used to match performance requirements. At the same time querying across multiple machines requires a more sophisticated optimiser than on a single machine.

The optimiser needs to take account of network performance, and ideally to be able to allocate processing according to the load on the machines on the network.

How has the Query Optimiser been changed to optimise data access across multiple machines?

Update

Where data is replicated the method of update propagation must be determined. All copies could be amended concurrently or there could be a primary copy with the duplicates maintained from it at regular intervals. A third possibility, which in fact replaces replication, is that of 'snapshots'. A predefined query is performed at specified intervals and the resulting snapshot table is copied to the sites wishing to use it. Applications read this resulting table rather than accessing the original table or tables. This method is not however transparent to the application since any update must be through the original and not the snapshot. All three methods have major implications for locking strategy.

With some methods users do not always get up to the minute data. In many circumstances this may not be important.

When data is replicated what is the method of update propagation?

If snapshots are used can the frequency of taking the snapshot be set by the database administrator?

67

Deadlocks

Global deadlocks must be identified and resolved. These are deadlocks involving transactions on more than one machine, since neither machine can easily identify what has happened, they must cooperate and transmit data to each other regarding transactions for which they are waiting.

The distributed database administrator must be aware of the implications of the consequences of hardware failures.

How are global deadlocks identified and resolved? What happens if one machine, or the communications, go down whilst holding locks across machines?

Concurrency

On a single machine the DBMS has the task of ensuring that different overlapping transactions, each of which are making changes to more than one table, are processed correctly and that data integrity is maintained. This process is known as concurrency. This problem is magnified when the coordinating DDM has to ensure that transactions which involve updates to table on more than one other machine each of which is under the control of a different DDM are correctly applied and data integrity is maintained across the distributed database. The distributed database manager (DDM) must have a clear concept of what constitutes a success unit. A process known as two phase commit strategy is employed, with the coordinating DDM requesting and obtaining confirmation of readiness from the DDMs at all nodes involved before issuing the instruction to commit. In the event of an intermediate failure the local DDM could adopt several different strategies:

- maximise correctness, where they hold the lock awaiting advice from the coordinating machine as to what action to take

- maximise availability, where an assumption must be made as to the expected outcome, normally assuming 'do it'

- rollback the update, where the entire system assumes that if any DDM fails to confirm that it has fully complied with the coordinator then all transactions should be undone, requiring a further two phase commit process.

Using such locking strategy greatly increases the network traffic and cannot ensure that the data is always correct. Potentially systems could allow users to disable the locking where performance is critical.

It is important that the functioning of the system is fully understood by the distributed database administrator. Note that it is vital, although difficult, to distinguish between actual capability of a product, and the claimed capabilities to which it aspires (and which its vendors will no doubt develop in time).

Does the product use a two phase commit?

What strategy is adopted in the event of hardware failure? How are the effects of such failure minimised?

Catalogue

The distributed database must keep a record (a catalogue) of where the data is stored and its format (metadata: data about data). There are three main ways of storing this metadata:

- centralise - record all the schemas etc in one location

- fully replicated - keep copies of the central catalogue at all nodes (one copy may be the primary copy)

- distributed - record the catalogue as a distributed database. Appropriate levels of replication and fragmentation must be determined

- partitioned - each site retains only a copy of the catalogue entries for its own tables.

Which alternative or combination thereof is preferable is largely dependent on how the database handles the issues outlined above, and whether there is an overall policy of correctness or availability. Performance can be affected greatly.

Usually relational database catalogues are themselves relational databases. This concept can be extended to distributed database catalogues being distributed databases. Therefore they are subject to the same considerations as described in the criteria above.

Where are the data definitions (schema or catalogue) stored?

Tuning

It is probable that in the longer term, good distributed database products will offer a selection of methods for handling these issues in the same way that selections of indexing methods are available today. This will enable the distributed database administrators (DDBA) to meet the system requirements. The DDBA will need to be a highly skilled individual (or team) to ensure that not only do the local network nodes operate efficiently and effectively, but that the network as a whole does so as well.

The DDBA will need greater awareness of hardware, particularly communications networks, than is normally required for a DBA.

What additional facilities are there for the DDBA to tune a distributed database?

What additional training will be required for the DDBA?

Gateways

In many cases there will be a requirement to run the new distributed database alongside an existing database and to be able to access data from it. This access is commonly referred to as a gateway. The capability of gateways is largely dependent on the type of existing database and its compatibility with the distributed database. If both are SQL-based then updates, inserts and deletes through the gateways should not be difficult to achieve. If the existing product is a network or hierarchical DBMS then the best that is likely at present is to obtain a relational view of the data in the database for read only purposes.

If the vendor cannot provide a gateway it may be possible for the project to build their own.

What gateways are available?

Chapter 6
Data distribution

Can the DBMSs accessed only be read, or can data be inserted, updated or deleted?

Are tools available to enable the project to build their own gateways?

Networks

In the same way that some databases are restricted to particular hardware some distributed databases are limited to particular networking protocols.

For full interconnectivity the product should not be so restricted.

What networking protocols are supported?

Can the product operate across ISO OSI-compliant networks? Do these comply with the Government OSI Profile (GOSIP)?

7 Structured Systems Analysis and Design Methodology

The use of SSADM is widespread in both private and public sectors. These users do not wish to introduce a different range of techniques and procedures for each DBMS they use because that would compromise their standards, reduce protection of investment and generally increase long term costs.

With this in mind CCTA has recommended to government departments that they contractually require suppliers to provide guidelines on how best to use their products with SSADM. This guidance should address all aspects of the product, including documentation and training The detailed objective of this CCTA policy is to:

- reinforce the fact that analysis and logical design still need to be conducted rigorously and in a controlled way irrespective of the implementation vehicle

- allow a smooth transition from logical to physical design without gaps, duplication or damaging compromise of requirements

- make full use of SSADM requirements and design deliverables - particularly in a turnkey or facilities management situation

- produce good quality documentation for the maintenance, future enhancement and eventual replacement of the system.

SSADM is presented and documented as an integrated set of structural, technical and documentation standards. The assessment of supplier support for their product in a project using SSADM should be assessed against all three criteria.

7.1 Compatibility

The rigour of SSADM should not be compromised and the following section explores the extent to which the guidance from the DBMS suppliers is compatible with SSADM.

The purpose of the SSADM analysis phase is to analyse and document the user requirement without the constraints imposed by any particular implementation choices. This logical view is encapsulated in the following techniques, which should not be changed for use with the DBMS:

- Data Flow Diagramming (DFD)

- Logical Data Structuring (LDST)

- Security, Control and Audit (SCA)

- User Options (USOP)

- Entity Life Histories (ELH)

- Relational Data Analysis (RDA)

- Composite Logical Data Design (CLDD).

Is there a tailored form of the SSADM Task List to lead the practitioner through the method, in a way compatible with the NCC Reference Manual, indicating any modified techniques?

The guidance should describe the use of standard SSADM end-products and techniques with the modified techniques and end products designed to maximise the usefulness of the DBMS. The guidance will be of little value if it cannot be quality assured with the standard SSADM document set.

Are there supporting descriptions of the cross-referencing and quality assurance of the modified end products to assist the smooth and effective operation of SSADM Reviews?

First-cut design rules define the mapping of the logical data design to a physical implementation, and this may be done as part of the Technical Options activity, as well as in the physical design stage of the method. In this stage, the design is tested against performance objectives, and tuned. Suppliers are well-placed to provide these rules.

Is there a set of First-cut Data Design rules, and if not, what is to be done?

Chapter 7
SSADM

Is guidance available on tuning the data design?

SSADM is an evolving standard and suppliers of DBMSs should be prepared to commit themselves to supporting new versions as and when they become available.

Does the DBMS supplier intend to support future versions of SSADM?

7.2 Tool support of SSADM

If an analyst workbench is used, then it is likely that the results of the SSADM analysis will be stored within a data dictionary, analyst workbench or CASE tool. The vendor may then supply tools that take analysis information from the dictionary or tool and automatically convert this into application outlines or even program code. The availability and sophistication of such tools is likely to have a significant impact on productivity.

In the assessment of such tools, the following points should be considered:

- the use of an integrated data dictionary to record the results of SSADM Analysis Phase activities and cross check them with DBMS design activities

- the use of an integrated, close or loose coupled, analyst workbench to produce SSADM end-products

- the ability of the tools to produce SSADM requirements documentation for the maintenance phase of the life cycle

- the SSADM Tools Conformance Appraisal Scheme is now in place, which will test CASE tools' level of conformance to SSADM on a four point scale. The scheme is administered jointly by CCTA and the SSADM Research Centre (SRC) at Birmingham Polytechnic.

Are there tools available to map from analyst workbench or CASE tools into database definition? Do such tools include links from the results of SSADM analysis?

Do such tools have any SSADM conformance scheme approval?

8 Product credibility

Database management systems are frequently the subject of 'imaginative' marketing. Some DBMS's are produced by small or relatively unknown software houses or are written and supported in foreign countries and marketed here by agents. Other DBMS's are new to the market-place and are therefore as yet untried. Such DBMS's are not necessarily of poor quality, but it is necessary to assess the likelihood of the software and the marketing agency still being viable in the future before committing to using the product, irrespective of its technical merit.

8.1 Quality of product

Database management systems should be constructed to a high quality using rigorous, structured development and testing techniques.

Is the product specified using a formal definition language or method such as VDM or Z?

Does the product developer subscribe to and comply with the requirements of British Standard (BS) 5750 or equivalent documents? (This deals with a supplier's capabilities to operate a quality management system in the design, manufacture, installation, inspection and testing of a product).

Has the product been submitted to any independent authority (eg the National Computing Centre Ltd (NCC)) for evaluation or certification/validation? If so, are the results available? Are any independently reached performance figures available from such authorities?

What guarantees are there against defects in the product?

8.2 Product development status

Information on the development status of the product is essential before making a long term commitment to its use.

What is the current development stage of the product, for example:

- *static?*

- *stable but in the process of being cosmetically enhanced (ie minor changes and improvements in presentation, or the way(s) in which the product interacts with the user, are in preparation but any such changes will not affect basic, user functions)*

- *being functionally enhanced?*

- *in the process of being developed for use on other machines?*

Have any enhancements been introduced recently? Are there any which are under development? If so, please list planned enhancements and the target dates for the introduction of such enhancements.

When was the last major, new version (as defined by the supplier) released and when is the next major, new version planned for release.

How does the company determine when a system requires enhancement and the nature of the additional or supplementary facilities and features which are to be incorporated?

Are there any weaknesses which have been identified in the current version of the product?

What plans are there for the product over next 3 to 5 years? Will the product be different to today's version? If so, what differences will there be?

How is system updating arranged to take account of new developments and legislation?

Have any overseas products been Anglicized (eg date format, £ symbol)?

How many updates have been issued in the last year?

8.3 Supplier assessment

The supplier assessment will take into account the size of the supplier, whether they are the originators of the software or simply agents, how long they have been producing or marketing software, the size and whether they are a company based in Britain or abroad.

Some DBMS's are produced originally by small independent software houses and then marketed, sometimes under another name, by computer manufacturers. This section should help to identify such products. Also, products simply marketed rather than developed by a supplier are likely to enjoy a lower level of on-going support.

Name, address and telephone number of supplier.

Name(s), position(s), address(es) and telephone number(s) of the person(s) to contact for further details, if necessary, regarding

- *Marketing information*
- *Technical support.*

How long has the company been in operation

- *in the UK?*
- *world-wide?*

Was the product originally developed by the above supplier?

What organisations have used the supplier's services in the past?

Does the supplier have a range of products covering related topics, ie is it an area in which he specialises?

Is the supplier a subsidiary of any other company? If so, please give details.

How many years has the supplier been active in the development and/or marketing of database management systems?

During the last year, what percentage of total revenue has been derived from database management systems?

How many employees are dedicated to the development of database management systems?

What percentage of total profit or income has been contributed to research and development of DBMSs? (ie future facilities, CASE, etc)

8.4 Product background

Most database management systems start their life in a slightly unstable state; some never achieve stability.

If a DBMS has a reasonable number of production field sites (not simply copies out for approval or copies distributed but not seriously used), then the product's capabilities and potential may be assumed to be at least adequate and the risk involved in selecting such a product is less than that of a new and untried package. New releases of a product however may be potentially risky.

Development ancestry
Potential buyers should establish when the 'product' was first available rather than the concept. Some database management systems are developments of tools used internally by the supplier. Sometimes these early internal versions are quoted to imply that the product has a better 'history' than is the case.

When was the DBMS first installed at a customer site for customer usage?

What is the source and history of product(s) under consideration?

For how long has the DBMS been commercially available?

What was the development environment (ie the machine on which the DBMS was developed in the supplier's organisation)?

Did the supplier write the DBMS, or is he acting as agent?

Where is the software originator based, eg local, UK, Europe, America?

Development profile
Many DBMS's are still in a state of development and enhancement. New features, facilities and environments are being added. While this may provide many useful new features it may cause problems if releases with desirable new features appear during a development.

Note. New versions of database management systems usually incorporate either significant improvements in functionality or in performance. New versions are typically released on an 18 to 24 month cycle. Intermediate releases tend towards fixing bugs only.

Chapter 8
Product credibility

How frequently are major product versions released? When was the last version released and when is the next one planned?

What enhancements, if any, are planned for the DBMS and when will they be introduced?

What is supplier policy towards compatibility between versions?

How does the DBMS supplier determine when a system requires enhancement and the nature of the additional/supplementary facilities which are to be incorporated?

Product usage
An indication of the numbers of users of the DBMS, the sales profile of the DBMS and other pieces of information such as product appraisal and evaluation reports can give a valuable insight.

How many user sites of the DBMS are there

- *in the UK?*
- *within Government?*
- *outside Government?*
- *elsewhere in Europe?*
- *elsewhere?*

How many systems of this type have been sold in the UK (and worldwide) during the past 12 months?

How many existing users are there (particularly any within government) and what is their volume of transactions (ie the number of applications currently in existence and use)?

For how long have earlier, or original, users stayed with the DBMS; or are all users (comparatively) recent?

Which is nearest competing product available in the marketplace?

Describe any previous projects using this DBMS with which the company has been involved both inside and outside of government. Please indicate the size and complexity of the jobs in broad terms.

81

Please give the name and address of reference site(s) which may be contacted if necessary.

Can other users be contacted, ideally in the same business area?

When was the first system of the type being considered (or proposed) successfully installed at a customer's site? Please provide details of the site's location and others, if available.

Does a user group exist for the product in question? If so, please state:

- *whether it was formed independently of the supplier's organisation*
- *how long such a group has been in operation*
- *how active it is*
- *the number of active members*
- *joining/ membership fees*
- *the number of meetings held each year*
- *when and where meetings are held?*
- *the name, address and telephone number of the group's secretary.*

How closely does the company collaborate with any such user groups which might be established?

Product information	Other sources of information other than those suggested by the product supplier can be valuable.

Are there any independent reports and evaluations on the DBMS(s) being considered? Can copies of any reports be made available? (IF NOT, WHY NOT?)

User Profile	While many DBMS's are usable by a wide class of users, most products are best suited to particular user profiles. Best results will always be attained when the correct tools have been chosen for the particular user profile. Most suppliers will claim usability by all classes of user.

Who are expected to be the principal users of the DBMS?

- *non IT staff*

- *analysts*
- *novice programmers*
- *experienced programmers*
- *others (please specify).*

8.5 Documentation

Database management systems require adequate documentation. Frequently DBMS's at the beginning of their life, or DBMS's marketed by small organisations, appear with inadequate documentation. Other DBMS's appear with large amounts of poorly structured documentation.

What information is available about the DBMS before purchase?

What documentation is available, and how well is it presented?

What manuals and other documentation are provided when the DBMS is purchased?

What other 'optional' manuals are available?

Can the documentation be copied by the user for his own use only?

What is the target audience for each manual eg management overview, system designer, application programmer, operator, etc?

Are the manuals available online?

What information is available on the technical content of the system, eg:

- *record formats*
- *database structure*
- *parameter tables*
- *validation mechanisms*
- *source code?*

In the event of the supplier going out of business, what arrangements are there for access to the source code, eg is a copy of the source code lodged with an Escrow Agent?

Is the customer to use the documentation provided or is there a need to develop instructions which are specific to each installation?

8.6 Training

Application generator packages in particular usually claim to require relatively small amounts of training, but this is not always the case. Poor quality training will predispose staff against good products and may therefore affect a project's overall success. Note that length of training required is not a sufficient guide as this will depend on the complexity of the product.

Note that DBMS's suitable for end-user use may require separate introductory courses for programmers and non-programmers.

Please state whether training is included in the purchase price of the proposed software system and:

- *where such training is normally carried out*
- *whether on-site courses can be arranged*
- *the nature and amount of training normally required to operate and use the DBMS (based on the company's previous experience)*
- *the duration of training courses*
- *the individuals at which such training is aimed.*

Are appropriate training courses provided by the supplier?

Do any third parties offer training in the use of the DBMS?

How much computing expertise is required by attendees?

Please describe any additional training related to the efficient and effective use of the system including details of cost, location, duration and frequency.

8.7 Support

Support will be required, especially when a DBMS is first introduced and before the organisation has built

Chapter 8
Product credibility

up its own in-house expertise. The type and level of support available will depend on the size of the supplier organisation and the number of sites they are supporting. There have been a number of instances where DBMS's have enjoyed rapid market success but this has resulted in their support services being thinly stretched or staffed by poorly qualified personnel. Support quality is also likely to be dependent upon where software development is done. If all development is done overseas, then the local knowledge of the internals of the software is likely to be reduced and the time taken to fix bugs increased.

Some DBMS's are purchased or marketed by UK suppliers, but not written by them. Where this is the case the level of UK support may be found wanting for newly established DBMS's.

General

Where and by whom is support undertaken?

Where are the support services located?

What is the policy for supporting previous releases of the DBMS and how many versions are currently supported?

To what extent is modification by users allowed without affecting support?

How are queries and problems dealt with after installation?

For which aspects of the implementation will the supplier be responsible (eg hardware and software installation, system and data conversion, user training)?

Pre-sales

Is a demonstration available?

What are the arrangements for a trial of the DBMS?

Does the right exist to reject the product if it fails user specified acceptance tests?

Will any verbal claims and promises made by sales people be written into the standard contract?

Who will provide support/answer queries, and how accessible are they, eg by telephone, office hours only?

ISE Appraisal and Evaluation
Database Management Systems Volume

Installation | What maintenance and support services are available during installation of the DBMS?

Will specific personnel be allocated to this project (full time/part time; at the beginning of, during and after implementation)?

Type and level | What maintenance and support services are available once the DBMS is operational?

How many technical support staff are supporting how many users?

How many technical support staff are available in the UK?

Does your company operate a 'hot-line' service for urgent user enquiries and fault reporting? If so, is the service part of a system maintenance agreement and please state:

- the average response time

- the longest response time

- the way in which the system operates.

How long does it take for a supplier's hot-line to answer, and how long to resolve queries?

Is there a charge for hot-line support?

What procedures are available for reporting problems and what action and priorities are assigned to rectifying faults?

Describe the circumstances in which on-site maintenance/ assistance would be given. Would such services be provided by a sales representative or by a software expert/engineer? What would be the contractual response time for a call for assistance?

Fault correction | Are details of system faults and required corrections circulated regularly to users? Is the software supplied with all corrections applied or are the corrections (fixes) supplied separately for incorporation by the user?

How are faults corrected (for example, by means of a new software issue; letter of notification; on-site assistance; or by telephone contact)?

Chapter 8
Product credibility

Are new versions of the DBMS automatically sent to users?

What are the escalation procedures for fault correction? When will the Managing Director become aware of a serious fault?

8.8 Enhancements

The methods and procedures by which enhancements to software products are handled are extremely important in the context of reducing or avoiding disruption during the introduction of enhancements or improvements to the package.

What arrangements can be made for future changes which may be required by the user?

What are the arrangements for future changes in requirements, and how will the work be costed?

How upward compatible is the AG for changes to

- *the hardware?*
- *the operating system?*

Are there facilities for users to 'customise' the AG?

ISE Appraisal and Evaluation
Database Management Systems Volume

9 Utilisation of recent technical developments

Information Technology is an area of rapid technological change and this applies, in no small measure, to database systems. This chapter discusses factors additional to those covered in previous chapters. It relates to the potential of the product to make use of likely hardware and software technical developments.

9.1 Hardware and system integrated DBMSs

Choice of a particular software vendor may well restrict availability to utilise potential technical developments that may become available. Possibly the easiest to consider is hardware assistance for database management systems. Several manufacturers already supply a DBMS with their hardware. Third party software vendors will find it increasingly difficult to match the performance characteristics of DBMS software directly supported by the hardware vendors. Note that hardware dependence is often inversely related to portability.

DBMSs are naturally quite intensive users of CPU resources. One way to improve CPU throughput is to move some of the database processing out of the main CPU. Three particular options exist for distributing the processing load of DBMSs.

Can the DBMS be supported directly by

- *specific DBMS machine hardware?*
- *intelligent peripheral controllers?*
- *conventional hardware, operating as a 'back-end processor'?*

9.2 Multi processor hardware

One approach to producing greater hardware performance is to employ multiple, parallel, processors.

To take advantage of such an architecture the DBMS needs to be able to divide its tasks and applications across the processors (note that CCTA is not, currently, implying a need for DBMS support of such devices).

Does the DBMS internal architecture support multi processor 'back-ends'?

9.3 Client/server

The benefits of separating the client (front-end application) from the server (back-end DBMS) are now becoming generally accepted. To provide these benefits the DBMS must have a clean separation between front-end and back-end, together with an efficient communication protocol and language.

Does the product support a 'clean' separation of front-end from back-end?

What protocol and language are used between front-end and back-end?

Chapter 10
System development and productivity tools

10 System development and productivity tools

The ability of a DBMS environment to support a range of development tools (either as an integral part of the DBMS product suite, as 'add on' products, or as software from an independent software vendor) is an important aspect of evaluation. In particular it should be noted that some major DBMS vendors are currently quite weak in their provision of high level development tools, although such tools are available from 3rd party software vendors. This is especially likely to be true if the DBMS in question conforms to open systems standards, in particular the database language SQL.

Note that this chapter should be ignored if a separate assessment of the development environment is being undertaken.

10.1 Application generator capabilities

AGs vary significantly in the type of systems that they are capable of developing. In particular, many AG products have limited capabilities for the development of batch systems, concentrating mainly on the development of on-line systems. Other products may impose restrictions such as complexity of screens or the type of transaction that can be constructed. For more detailed assessment of AG tools see the AG Appraisal and Evaluation Volume.

Is there an AG integral with the DBMS or is it a separate product?

Is there a choice of AGs which may be used with the DBMS?

Can the AG make full use of the capabilities of the DBMS?

10.2 Integration with development tools

The better development environments consist of an integrated set of tools, including a fourth generation language, a data dictionary, testing and documentation facilities. Ideally, these are tightly coupled in that they share objects such as definitions. Such integration is less likely to be guaranteed if the development tool software is provided a number of by 3rd party software vendors.

ISE Appraisal and Evaluation
Database Management Systems Volume

Query facility
: Investigate availability of interactive query facilities provided by, or compatible with, the DBMS. Such a facility may be of use both to service application requirements and to act as a programmer(s) debugging tool. Some self contained systems will have an Interactive Query Facility (IQF) as an integral part of the language.

Is the IQF included within the cost of the DBMS and is it an optional extra component or a separate product?

Query languages for non DP personnel probably have an English-like syntax and may not require the user to have an intimate knowledge of the database structure. Few IQFs are really suitable for general use by non DP personnel but forms interfaces may be available.

Is the IQF designed for use by programmers or by non DP personnel (end users)?

What type of interface is there between the IQF and the user?

Report writer
: Investigate the availability of report writing facilities. Such facilities, if comprehensive, can significantly reduce the time taken to produce reports.

Some self contained systems will have report writing capabilities as an integral part of the system. For a host language DBMS, the report writer will probably be an associated product.

Does the DBMS include a report writer facility?

Is the report writer included within the cost of the DBMS and is it an optional extra component or a separate product?

Report writers for programmers usually require detailed knowledge of the database structure and frequently have non trivial syntax. Few complex reports can be produced by non DP personnel, although simple reports often can be.

Is the report writer designed for use by programmers or by non DP personnel?

Chapter 10
System development and productivity tools

	Reports can usually be specified more conveniently interactively.
	Are reports specified interactively or in a batch mode?
Application development facility	The type, efficiency and ease of use of application development facilities in particular, application generators, can have a significant effect on project timescales and costs. Most major database systems have some form of AG associated with them. If their usage is likely to be significant, the separate AG Appraisal and Evaluation Volume should be consulted.
	Many self contained systems claim to have some form of facility which is termed an 'application generator' or a 'fourth generation language'. Major host language systems have associated products, sometimes available from 3rd party software vendors
	Does the DBMS include any applications development facilities?
	Is the applications development facility included within the cost of the DBMS, is it an optional extra or is it a separate product?
	Application generators are more likely to support only the development of on-line systems. Facilities such as the report writer may cater for a significant component of batch application requirements.
	Is the applications development facility capable of developing batch and/or on-line applications?
Data dictionary	Data dictionary facilities are highly desirable for any significant database development. Dictionaries which are integrated with the DBMS are more likely to be 'active' rather than 'passive' retainers of information.
	Most commercially significant DBMS are supported by some form of dictionary. For some systems it is an integral part or a necessary additional component.
	Is the DBMS supported by a data dictionary system? Is the dictionary a prerequisite?

The data dictionary should contain elements corresponding to the entities which comprise the database schema. Also, it is usually necessary to be able to document several schemas, including multiple versions of a schema.

Is the data dictionary capable of containing both development and operational versions of the logical database description (schemas), data views (subschemas) and process information?

For significant system developments, a data dictionary is a necessity. Comprehensive dictionary facilities may be expensive. For some systems, dictionaries from third party software vendors may be available.

Is the data dictionary facility included within the cost of the DBMS, is it an optional extra component or is it a separate product?

If the data dictionary is an external product it is important that it can interface well with the DBMS.

If a separate product, how does the data dictionary generate the DBMS schema?

How are changes propagated?

Can a data dictionary definition be 'reverse engineered' from an existing DBMS schema?

It is desirable that the data dictionary to be used is acceptable for all system documentation. This includes documentation of conventional (non database) files and analysis documentation.

In addition to DBMS related data what other information can the dictionary be used to maintain?

- *information about conventional files*
- *results of analysis (models etc)*
- *other.*

10.3 3GL development support

Effective development of database systems in a 3GL environment requires tools such as test database

Chapter 10
System development and productivity tools

generators, test harnesses for modules and batch terminal simulators for testing TP environment programs.

What specific facilities are available for application development in a 3GL environment?

10.4 Development cycle support

It is commonly recognised that the analysis, design, construction and maintenance of computer systems are an integrated set of tasks and that they should be supported by common tools; in particular, data dictionaries and more recently, analyst and programmer workbenches. Of these, integrated dictionary support is probably the most significant and in a Government project environment this almost certainly implies the need for the dictionary to support the Government analysis and design methodology SSADM.

Data dictionaries are a technology that is in place and proven today. Workbenches are an emerging but advancing technology, and are likely to be significant in reducing system development costs in the near to medium term. In the longer term, facilities promised such as 'automatic systems generation' are likely to be significant but these are not currently widely available and many claimed systems are currently in their infancy.

What development cycle support tools are available to be used with the DBMS?

Program test aids

Aids to help programmers debug their programs are desirable in a database environment to improve programmer productivity.

Identify the aids which exist. Options which may be available include:

- end of job statistics

- DB call traces

- DB exception handling routines

- DB print programs.

What aids exist to facilitate program testing?

The facilities may be restricted in an on line environment. Some systems provide batch testing facilities for on-line transactions. This, if provided, would probably be an additional software component available at extra cost.

Can these facilities be used for both batch and on-line applications?

10.5 End user tools

It is useful to differentiate between tools for the data processing professional and tools for the non professional. Many relational DBMS vendors claim that their native database language is suitable for end users. In practice this is unlikely to be true; native database languages invariably require a knowledge of a complex language syntax and often require a detailed knowledge of the database structure. Better end user tools allow a menu driven form filling approach to query or report specification and provide query views and synonyms to conceal the unnecessary complexity of the database structure from the occasional user.

What end user tools are available?

Does the end user need to know the database structure in order to use the available tools?

10.6 Data conversion, loading and migration tools

Conversion from the current system to new systems can be a difficult business. Some database systems have emulators to allow existing applications to run in an unmodified form, accessing converted data.

DBMS vendors also offer data conversion aids to help move data from one database environment to another.

If large volumes of data are to be loaded, then some form of database load utility is probably desirable, although not as necessary as in a network database environment.

Database loading

Initial loading of a large database, especially one with a pointer based storage architecture, can be a very long job. Often, utilities are provided which optimise this process. Such utilities provide the following types of facilities:

- build indexes only when all the base data has been stored

- store data without resolving pointers between data elements; the pointers being resolved and stored in a later phase.

Adding data to an existing database may be a requirement in the following circumstances:

- on additive database restructure

- on phased data takeon when initially loading a database.

Adding data to an existing database requires a slightly more sophisticated approach than placing data into an empty database.

What facilities exist to enable large volumes of data to be efficiently loaded when creating a database?

Can these facilities be used to add bulk data to an existing database?

11 Project specific requirements

Any other requirements specific to the Departmental IT Strategy and/or project but not fully covered in other parts of this volume.

12 Costs

Cost comparison, where cost benefit analysis allows for the value of the benefits the products bring, is performed in detail for the final selection of a product from the short list of approved products. However, there is also a case for including costing in the higher level formulation of the short list. For this purpose (i.e. software comparison), costing need not be done at a detailed or absolute level; approximate relative costs are sufficient.

12.1 Software

Software costs include a basic licence cost plus a recurrent annual maintenance charge. When prices are given it should be indicated whether these are inclusive or exclusive of VAT.

Is the product licensable only or can it be purchased?

How much does it cost to buy the product outright? Does this cost include a copy of the source code?

Does the product require any particular separately purchasable requisites?

How much does it cost to rent or lease the product

- *per month?*
- *per year?*

What are the minimum and maximum rental periods?

What are your terms for multiple copies of the product

- *on a single site?*
- *on multiple sites?*

Is an organisation wide licence available?

Data dictionaries or AG software will possibly also be necessary. These may or may not be included within the cost of the DBMS. Note also that some DBMSs have many selectable (and separately purchasable) components.

Are there any other software components not previously mentioned (from any vendor source) which are required?

A reasonable level of initial installation support is useful to help gain confidence in new techniques.

What installation support is included within the purchase price? Does the price include the cost of new versions?

Is any warranty provided?

Is software support provided? If so what is the cost?

12.2 Hardware

Hardware costs vary with different product sets. The existence of a TP monitor and of multi-threading software can reduce significantly CPU costs. If the product is to be installed on existing hardware, then enhancement of this hardware may be necessary.

As with software, hardware is likely to have an initial capital cost together with a recurrent maintenance cost. Costs may have to be considered for the system as a whole and not just the DBMS element.

What is the cost of enhancement of existing hardware (for example additional disc and/or memory) in order to support the product?

12.3 System development, operation and maintenance

System associated costs vary with the type of development tools used. 4GL tools will reduce development time and probably maintenance costs but will consume more hardware resources during development and operation. 3GL tools may produce efficient systems but take a long time to develop and may be more expensive and difficult to maintain. Different costs may be incurred depending on the type of licence, for example development or runtime. If purchasing the latter ensure that it includes all necessary facilities.

With certain types of product significant savings may be made by not purchasing unnecessary copies of development software (generators, editors, compilers, etc) in an environment where applications are run on multiple sites, but development is done centrally.

Chapter 12
Costs

What are the maintenance terms?

Can the product be acquired on a trial basis and if so for how long and what are the costs involved? Are these costs discounted from any subsequent purchase price?

Are runtime only copies of the product available? If so, what is the cost? And what is excluded?

12.4 People

People costs are affected by factors such as the number needed, training requirements and their commercial worth. Sophisticated development tools reduce the number of people required for application development and probably reduce the costs incurred in training. However, such trained people may be commercially attractive and require a high salary to retain them. Sophisticated tools are also likely to require skilled infrastructure support and such people are likely to be expensive. Take on of new technology may require outside consultancy support which, whilst sometimes cost effective, will be expensive.

What is the cost of any training not provided free of charge when the product is purchased?

What is the cost of any manuals not provided free of charge when the product is purchased?

Is consultancy support available from the vendor? If so, what is the cost?

Annex
Criteria hierarchy

Criteria hierarchy

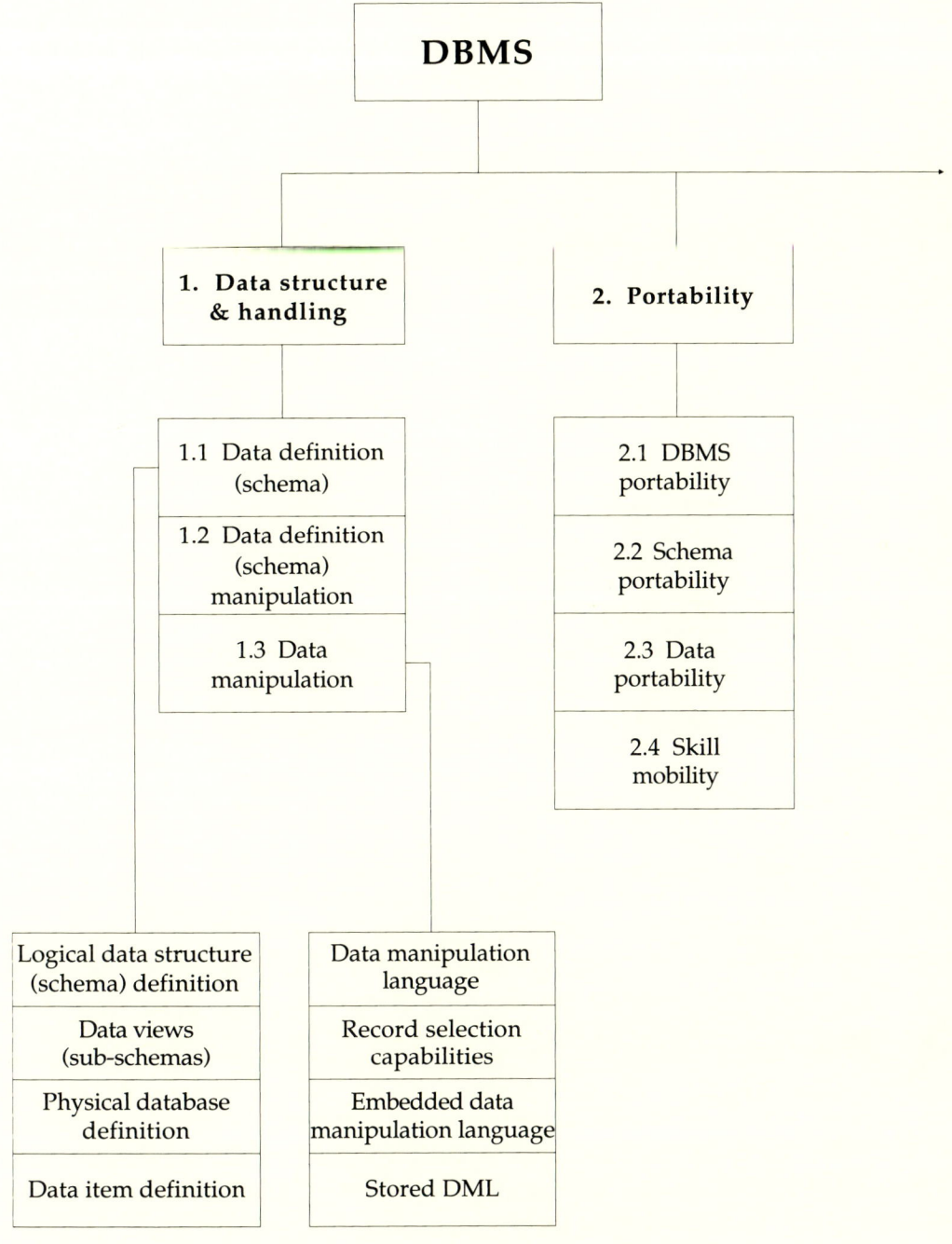

105

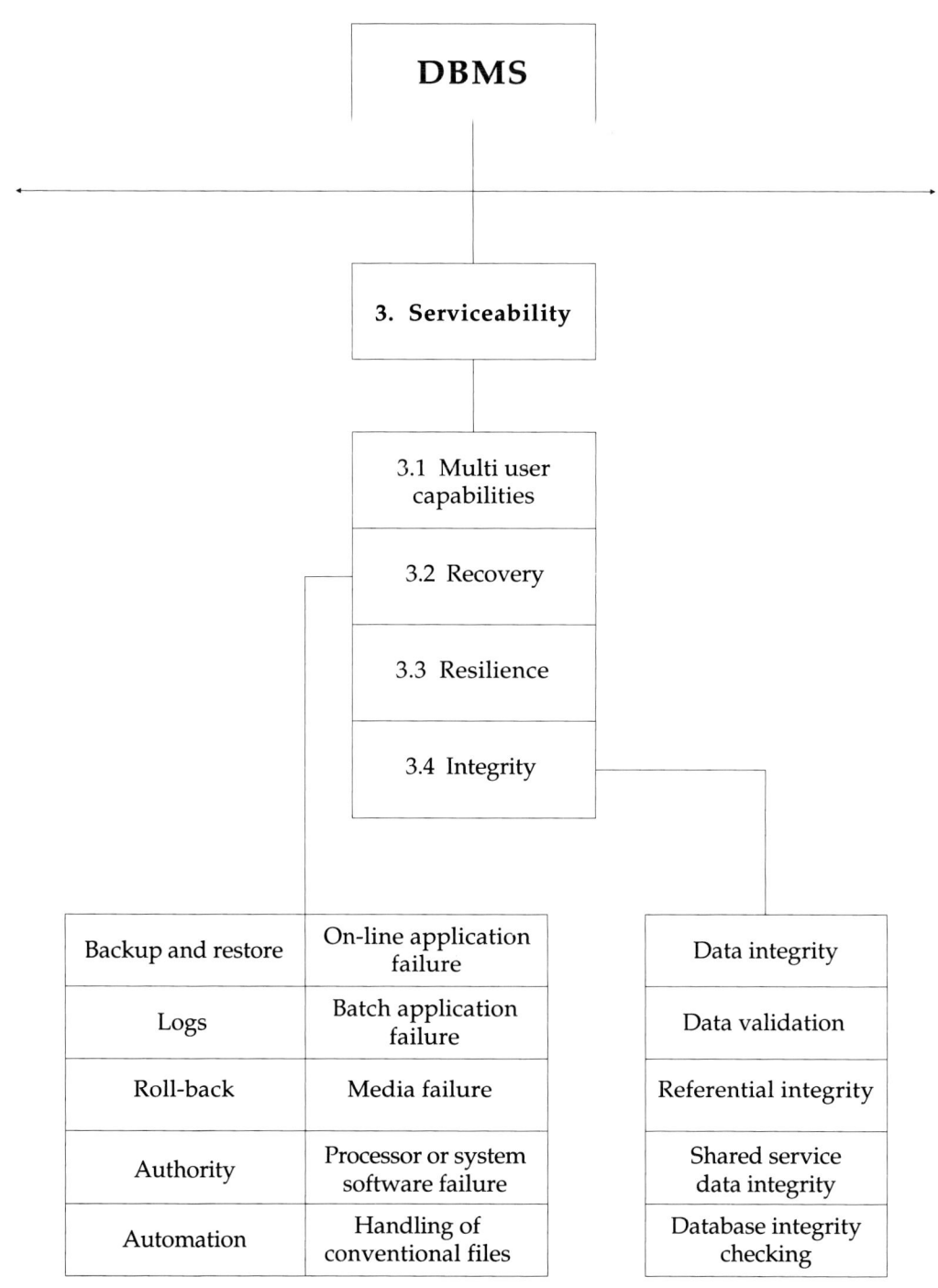

Annex
Criteria hierarchy

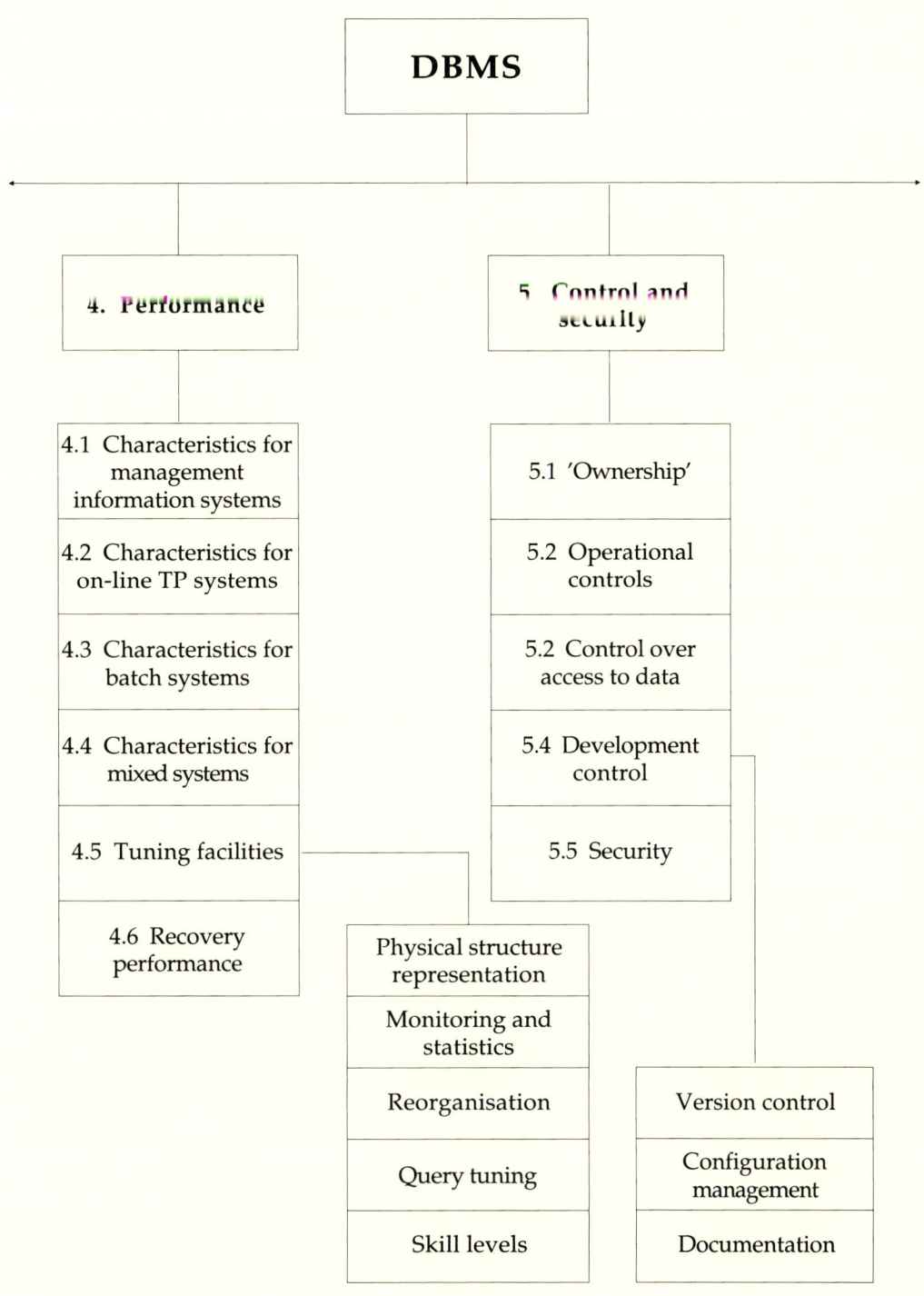

ISE Appraisal and Evaluation
Database Management Systems Volume

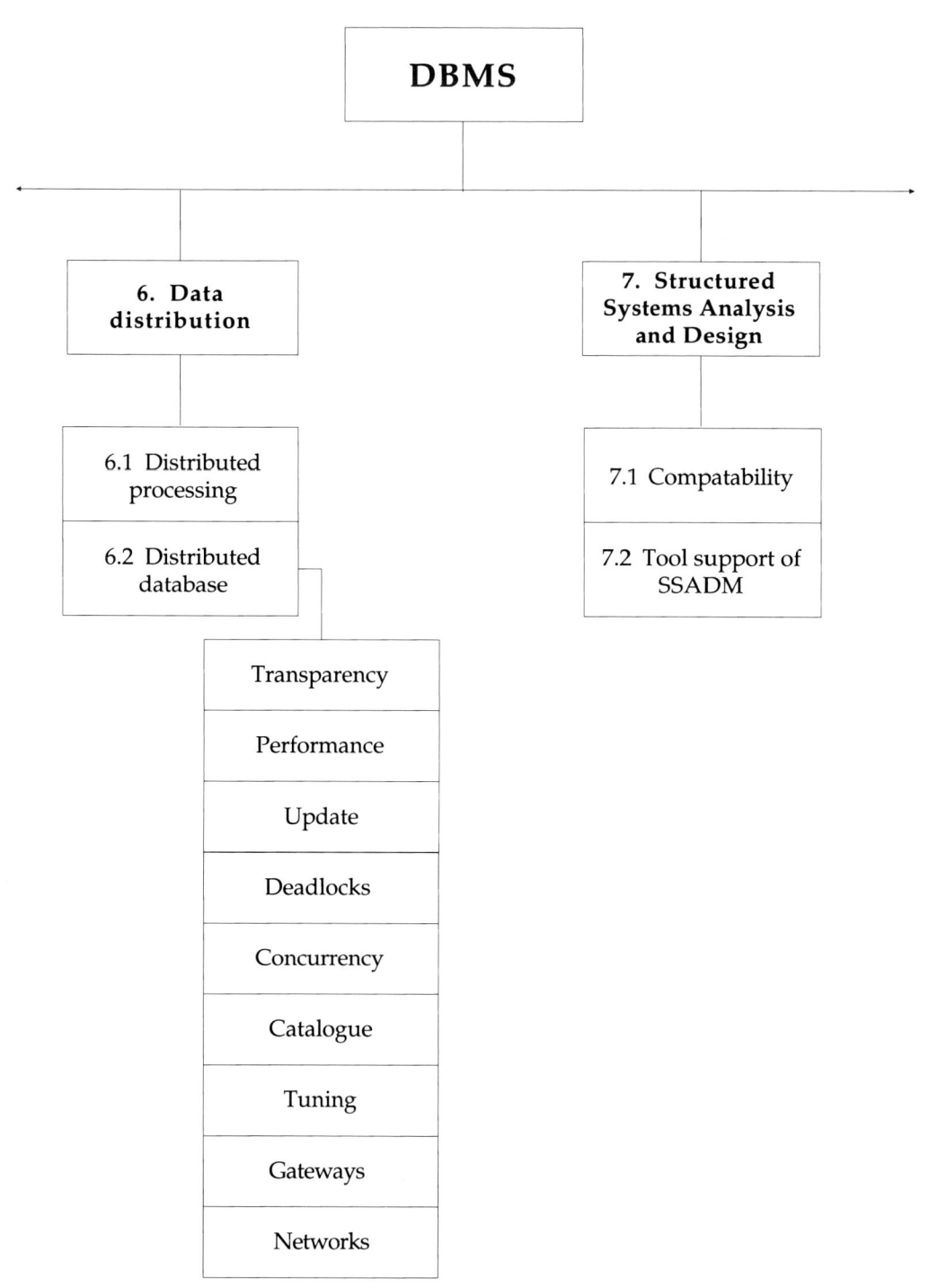

Annex
Criteria hierarchy

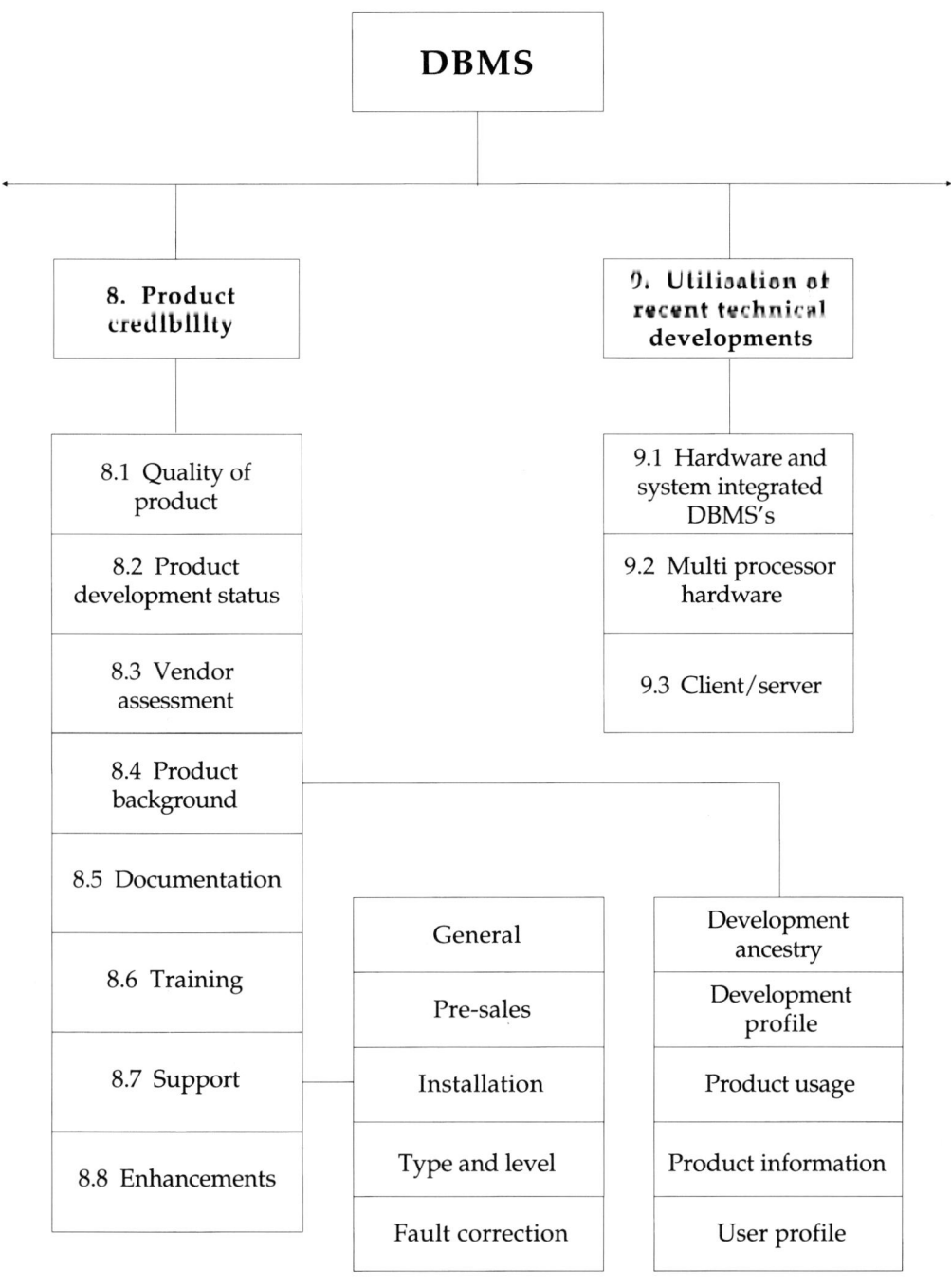

109

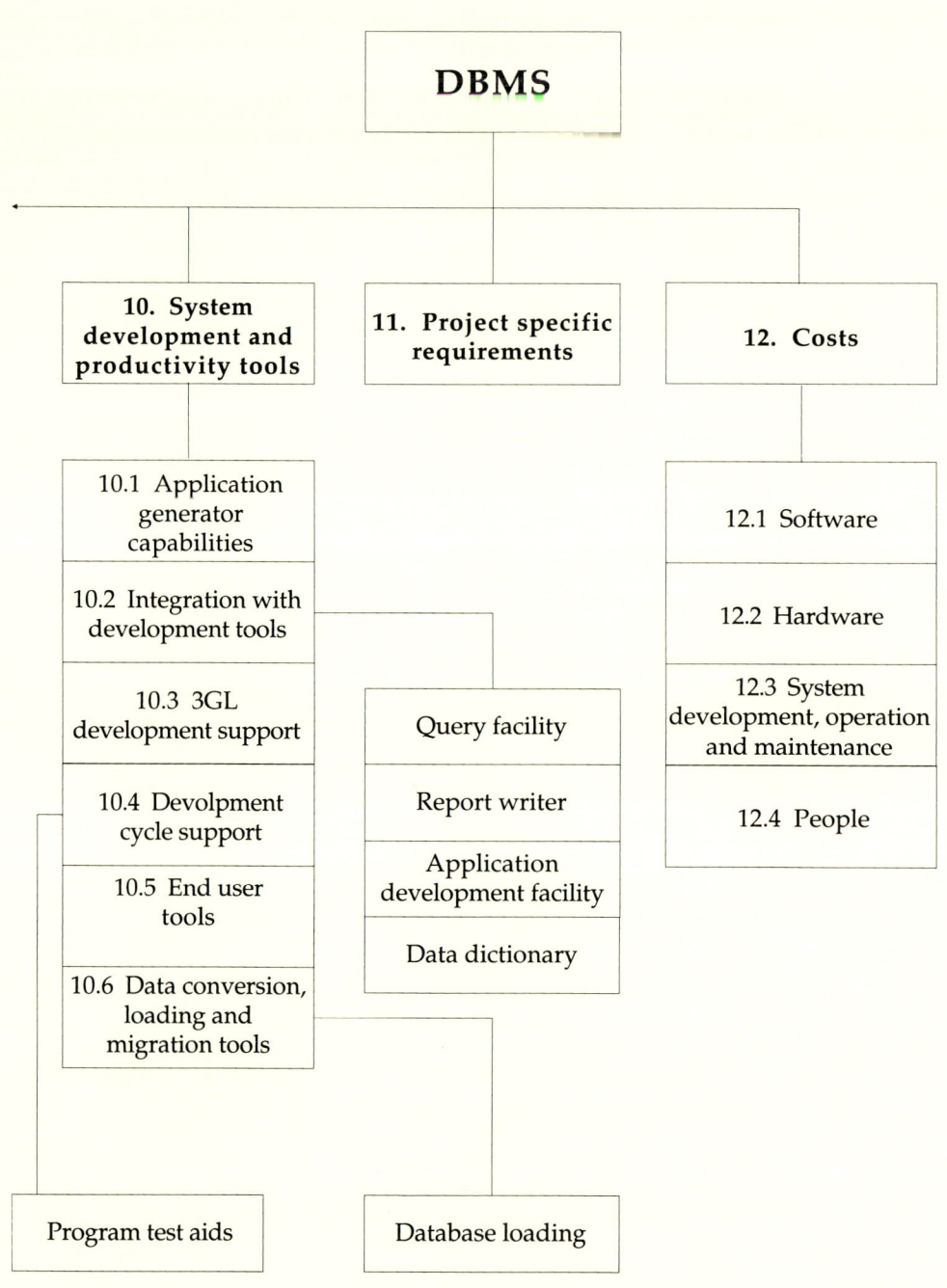